DERANGED

Finding a Sense of Place
in the Landscape and in the Lifespan

Jill Sisson Quinn

Apprentice House
Baltimore, Maryland
www.apprenticehouse.com

First Edition, revised
Printed in the United States of America

Paperback ISBN: 978-1-934074-60-2
Ebook ISBN: 978-1-934074-25-1

Illustrations by Cara Ober
Cover photo by Tom Quinn

Published by Apprentice House

Apprentice House
Loyola University Maryland
4501 N. Charles Street
Baltimore, MD 21210
410.617.5265 •410.617.2198 (fax)
www.ApprenticeHouse.com
info@ApprenticeHouse.com

Advance praise for "Deranged"

"Quinn's great achievement is that she not only tells a good story about growing up in Maryland, moving to Wisconsin with her husband, coming to terms with her infertility, and discovering her place in her new environment, but that she turns to nature—mayflies, honey bees, glacier-formed landscapes, ticks, and red maples to create symbols, to contextualize her speculations, to probe, deepen, and universalize her experiences, and to learn to live a richer, deeper life. Deranged belongs on the same shelf in my home library as works by Henry David Thoreau, John Muir, Annie Dillard, and Terry Tempest Williams. Deranged is beautifully conceived and beautifully written."

> – Lisa Knopp, author of *Interior Places*

"Quinn brilliantly combines scientific fact with personal experience, elevating both through the use of vivid imagery and lyrical language. The metamorphosis of maturation becomes something both strange and familiar as Quinn describes moments of displacement—that limbo of awareness that exists at the boundaries of change."

> – Kim Barnes, author of *In The Wilderness: Coming of Age in Unknown Country*

"Quinn writes in Dillard's footsteps, in the tradition of close observation wedded to a perceptual frame that's ruminative, so she belongs in the company of the best of the new-generation naturalists, writers such as Barbara Hurd. Lyrical and factual in equal measure, she writes like an angel taking field notes. When you read Quinn, you feel as though you're really with her—you're watching insect life or pond scum or a creek, or you're the wind that's blowing through her (she'll tell you exactly at what rate it's moving), or you're contemplating geological formations such as kames, or you're a visual predator seeking spring's first peepers, or you're checking your neck because her description of how ticks make you into a bloodmeal is that visceral."

> – Diana Hume George, author of *The Lonely Other: A Woman Watching America*

"Jill Quinn's work is close in spirit to Annie Dillard's. She describes topographical and biological phenomena in crystalline prose, and uses them as bases for deep meditation, both personal and philosophical."

> – Kevin Kerrane, editor of *The Art of Fact: A Historical Anthology of Literary Journalism*

"A trumpet. A bathtub. A big sister. A narrator who goes to investigate this congruence of incongruent things. The narrator is not forcing us to gaze upon her life and her experience; rather, she invites us to look with her, as comrades, at the common things that both startle and amaze. Quinn is a superb writer, with much to teach us."

> – Brenda Miller, Editor-in-chief, *Bellingham Review*

For Tom

Acknowledgements

The author gratefully acknowledges the publica-
tions where earlier versions of these essays first appeared,
sometimes under different titles:

Bellingham Review: "The Myth of My Childhood"
Crab Orchard Review: "Too Ridiculous to Remember"
Fourth Genre: "This Game"
Quarter After Eight: "Sugaring Off"
American Nature Writing 2003: "This Game,"
    "Watch the Cord," "How Fluid My Body,"
    and portions of the Introduction

Introduction

The Last Time

Falling in love for the second time can never be as good as the first—even though it may be better—simply because it was not the first. In the same way, developing a sense of place in a new land feels like resignation. I know it is adaptive to take on a new place as your own, in my case accepting a land that once threw me off balance with its sky-laden plains. But not to live in sorrow of a place you have left, not even the sorrow of forgetting it, which, I suppose, for me, is the next step, seems to nullify the belief that there is somewhere one belongs, the entire concept of home.

I have always been haunted by last times. Traversing a narrow woods trail that led through knee-high weeds from my parents' yard in Maryland to a neighbor's field, along which my sisters and I had set up camp—building a teepee, digging a fire pit and outlining it with rocks, swinging on vines and climbing trees—I used to sometimes suddenly wonder: When will be the last time I will walk this? I did not dwell on the question. It was a pause in some game. It was a revelation I took for granted and kept contained which might arise when I stopped to remove a burr from a shoelace, or unstitch a thorned branch from my sleeve. Perhaps because the path was so integral to my play, because it was difficult to believe that one day it would not be, but because even at that age I knew that nothing lasted forever, this question was able to surface. When it did, it hit me like a retracted twig. But mostly I kept it repressed, as humans do the immutable fact of their own deaths.

And there was a last time I walked that path. There must have been; the trail is not there anymore—though the wood is—but for the life of me, I can't remember it. Did it happen at the end of a summer or at the beginning? Did it mark an abrupt change? Did I use the path regularly up to a certain date and then never again? Or did I gradually use it less and less over the course of a whole season? When I stepped off that path for the last time, had it begun to grow over from disuse already, or was it still a clear avenue of dead leaves amidst the viney green on both its sides, the width of a child's hips?

Very rarely, you can be aware that something is happening for the last time as it occurs. A year or two after my grandmother died, my family ate spaghetti fully cognizant that it had been made from the last of her canned tomato sauce. Before dinner, my mother came up from the basement, holding the jar with its blood-red contents, and made a general announcement: This is the last of them. It was as if we were finally putting my grandmother to rest, eliminating from the world the last thing, except for our own bodies, that she had created. We ate, and some bit of energy that had flowed from the green thumb of my grandmother through those tomatoes grown in the soil of land she owned, boiled in pots in her kitchen, mashed by wooden spoons in her hands, flowed into me. I knew I would never be able to commune with her in this way again.

But the last time we connect with a person is different than the last time we connect with a place. Living things are expected to die. Terrible as it is, we know it from a young age. We fear it, or dread it—at least subconsciously—all our lives, and when it finally happens—as long as the death is not untimely—we have become accustomed to its inevitability; we accept it and grieve. But with a place it is different. I am not saying one is worse than the other, but that they are dissimilar. A place can change, sometimes drastically, but a place does not die or disappear. A place does not leave you. You leave it.

What saddens me most is not what I am missing by not living in the land of my youth, but how I forget, sometimes, what in the foothills of the Appalachians I used to desire: heavy, green, tree-covered mountains, which hid the firmament, skirted by rushing streams. I forget this when I am feeling fulfilled by the kind of vista the Midwest has to offer: more lines of cumulus clouds than I can count, like a farmer's rows of cauliflower bursting forth from the ocean rather than the soil, a picture that widens eyes with its soft colors.

Animals also have a strong sense of place. Some of them—especially birds—have quite an extraordinary one. Migration, in which birds fly between seasonal homes along the same path, can be amazing in itself; the Arctic tern travels nearly 25,000 miles twice a year, virtually from one pole to the other, a distance which makes the 800 miles I moved across the United States seem like a minor excursion. But a greater mystery than migration is the quality of "homing," or a bird's ability to return to its home from an unknown area over an unknown flight route.

Most people are familiar with the homing pigeon, a domestic bird used for sending and receiving messages to and from base camps in World War I. Interestingly, the rock dove, from which the homing pigeon was bred, is a non-migratory bird with very little homing ability. But if a homing pigeon can be bred from a virtually sedentary bird, all birds must exhibit homing to some degree, and terns, gulls, cowbirds, starlings, and swallows—some of which make their home in my back yard here in Wisconsin—can find their way back to their homes in astonishing circumstances.

In two early experiments, described in my *Audubon Nature Encyclopedia*, noddies and sooty terns were transported by steamship from the Tortuga Keys, a group of small islands between Florida and Cuba, to a variety of points they had never visited before along the Atlantic and Gulf coasts. For a human, getting to the Tortuga Keys, which are closer to Cuba than to the U.S., is a mind-numbing, 70 mile, three-hour ride in a catamaran from Key West, marked only by endless blue-green water. But a bird taken 585 miles away from the Tortugas returned to its nest in just under four days; one taken 855 miles away was back in just over six.

More fascinating than when the birds returned, however, is how they did it. At first, it was commonly thought that the birds were simply retracing the exact route used to take them away. They used either an "inner ear-guided" sense of direction, or visual cues, though the only "visual cues" my husband and I saw on our excursion to the Tortugas were the occasional dolphin or school of flying fish; it took us quite a while, even, to pick out the colored buoys put up by the park service to mark the trail. To disprove this theory, scientists gathered a sample of starlings, chloroformed them, placed them in boxes, and rotated the boxes on phonographs while the birds were transported from their homes. When the birds were awakened and released, even after this dizzying experience, nearly 100 percent found their way back to their nests. Another theory held that birds used a "magnet" located in their brains to follow the earth's natural magnetic fields. More ingenious scientists stepped in, releasing pigeons with strong magnets fastened beneath their wings in order to confuse them. Did they make it home? You bet, in spite of the extra weight.

My husband is getting tired of the line, "I moved to Wisconsin with my husband, who wanted to return to his home state." He is getting tired of my constant, glib contrasts: "In Maryland, none of the rivers flow north." I am wrong; the Youghiogheny does, on which I have even kayaked and rafted. My geographical confusion while looking over a bridge in Wisconsin at the falls of the Copper and Bad Rivers, both of which flow north into Lake Superior, has nothing to do with the imprint the Maryland watershed left on my brain, with which I claim the Wisconsin watershed clashes in a way that makes me feel crazy. Unlike the birds, I have no internal divining-rod-compass, formed from splashing in Maryland streams in my early years, whose red end points southeast toward the Chesapeake Bay. I'm like most people, who mistakenly believe it is out of character for a river to flow north. But just as many rivers flow north as they do east, west, and south. All rivers flow downhill, whatever direction that happens to be.

My husband is waiting for the last time I write about the incompetence of the Midwestern landscape from an Easterner's standpoint.

Although, in general, they excel at it, birds are not the only animals with homing ability. The *Audubon Nature Encyclopedia* claims that salamanders can find their way back to a favorite section of stream from up to one mile away. Even box turtles, according to D.M. Carroll in *The Year of the Turtle*, normally thought of as slow and clumsy travelers, have found their way back through unknown territory when released from one to two miles from their homes. In a 1998 *National Geographic* article on wolves, Douglas H. Chadwick writes about a female wolf in Montana which, after being implicated in killing a rancher's heifer, was drugged, taken 160 miles from her mate, and released, only to find her way back to her mate's territory, and the disgruntled rancher's property, in 11 days. In addition to fostering the ability to find their homes against great odds, these animals must also have an uncannily strong motivation to look for them, for they persevere even when the territories they are placed in could presumably meet their basic needs. They refuse, for any reason other than death, to see their homes for the last time. And sometimes, so do we.

More recently, scientists have posited that it is a combination of abilities, including magnetic sensing and navigation by the sun and stars that allows birds to home so efficiently. How odd that the simple stars, the objects that first led men away from their homes and into new worlds, turn out to be the clue that animals all over the globe are using to return to their homes, after being displaced and misplaced by humans, not in the experimental arena, but in the economic one. Perhaps that is where humans strayed, literally: passionately overdeveloping their skills in exploration and, as a consequence, losing the knack for getting home. Like

Odysseus, who sailed the sea for ten years before returning to the house where his wife and dog faithfully awaited him, we have covered the corners of the earth, discovered and uncovered all of her habitats, and now find ourselves desperately trying to recover them.

I cannot stop thinking of home. I do not wish to have felt "at home" for the last time. I like to imagine that my own sense, like the birds', is something grand that I am not fully conscious of, some science at work within me, leading me back to earth from the air and the sea. I like to believe that there is some un-faulty guide steering me home, and hope that if I am not there now, I soon will be.

When was the last Saturday morning my two older sisters and I spent on my middle sister's single bed, playing, after breakfast, in our pajamas, secret, silly, ritual games? I know those morning meetings of piled things, of skin and plush and blankets and imagination, of time un-tethered, of no parameters except for the edges of a twin mattress, most likely ended gradually. But I feel as if there must have been a Saturday when, after the last game, after my mother told us to get dressed for the last time, we walked away from that bed, arms outstretched, our limp hands and will-less eyes pulled by some uncontestable, invisible force, never to meet there again, directly into adulthood, into marriage and, for my sisters, into being mothers.

Like the terns whose empty nests, merely a ground scrape or hollow in the rocks, caked with seaweed, called to be filled from several hundred miles away, or the wolf which, alone in suitable territory, insisted on being with its mate, the drive to procreate, to raise young, is equally as strong as the drive to feel at home. And, for we humans, having children can deter the last times of things: the last time you were truly excited on Christmas morning, the last time you roasted a marshmallow, the last time you read Snow White or Cinderella, the last time you stopped to observe a single leaf falling into a river. Children seem to pull time into a circle.

When will be the last time I will mourn not being able to have children? It lessens as the years go by. Will I still feel it in the womb at age eighty-five, this pull of my absent progeny, the stirrings of an imagined, hoped-for child, the desire for my own flesh to navigate into this world again, violently denying that my own birth was the last of something?

Last times are a curious thing. They are easily missed. They often cannot come into existence until after they have happened, which makes you wonder if they exist at all. And last times can be quite ephemeral. They can lose their status in an instant—the moment you lay eyes on that one horizon you never thought you would see again, feel freshly that pain which now seems to have belonged to another person, you have made a new last time. And so many last times hinge on death, especially the death of a desire.

There was a time, when I first moved to Wisconsin, when a trail led me through a windbreak between two fields, a farmer's hedge, just a thin vein of woods. I moved through the line of trees like an invader circulating through some other organism's blood. But now, I have found my path: I begin at the end of this very trail and stop just short of the windbreak.

I begin at the end of the trail not because of my obsession with the ends of things, but because it puts you immediately on a narrow, winding, pine needle covered path that cuts up the side of a forested hill. You dip down and up five times until you have reached what feels like the center. You cannot see through the woods in any season, in any direction. I sit here on the steep, wooded banks of a deep glacial kettle whose bottom, fortunately for the spotted salamanders that spawn here in spring, dips just below the water table. I await the time when I can descend to the marshy edge to reach for their golf-ball-sized clusters of eggs, like giant eyeballs with too many pupils looking out at the world in all directions, the same I would find in vernal pools in the forests of Maryland. Here, I feel I've no danger of coming upon or becoming like that child who stepped from the woods into her parents' back yard never to return again. Here, amidst the trees and uneven ground, the tiny bodies of a hundred salamander larva gestating in my hands, I begin to feel a sense of place, a sense of purpose, the same I've always had. But it's a trick. Unlike the animals who home so well, who strive, at energy's great expense, to reproduce, this is the sense I have within me: who we are and what we call home are mutable. For here, as everywhere, there is another last time looming: this is the place where I will no longer desire the land of my youth, this is the time when I will leave behind my yearning to have a child. This is where I will only feel sad—and less and less sad with each walk—for forgetting them.

PART 1

Egg

[1] *The Myth of My Childhood*

Once every six months or so, when she was thirteen or fourteen, my sister would wash her trumpet. It was never announced; in fact, I only came upon it by accident. I noticed her kneeling by the tub, leaning out of view, as I walked down our hall, and slipped into the bathroom to investigate. In just two steps, I came upon an act so puzzling and awesome, at first I thought I had finally caught her, six years older and wiser than me, doing something she wasn't supposed to be doing. After all, the bathtub was for washing living things. Even our dog we washed with a hose in a plastic tub in the yard. I may have protested and been rebuked, had the occasion sullied by her to something I was finding out second-hand, as usual, but I remember no dialogue between the two of us. In fact, because of the trumpet, it felt like there were three of us in the room, but because the trumpet was under water, we were all muted.

The whole scene was confusing. Each object in view

hovered far from its usual purpose. A pink towel had been folded and placed on the bottom of the tub. I assume now it was to keep the trumpet from scratching the porcelain, or the porcelain from altering the flare of the trumpet's bell. But at that time my eyes fixed on this towel beneath the water, as if it were our only one; how would she dry the trumpet with a wet towel, I wondered? And then, lying on its side upon the towel, soaking, was the instrument itself, slightly magnified, completely submerged. The brass was shiny as ever; why did it need to be washed? The piano in our living room, which I played, sometimes needed to be dusted, but never bathed.

Almost more visible than what was there, was what was missing. Where was the trumpet's case? It was not in the room. At first, I imagined the trumpet had walked to the bath itself. Finally, I decided that it had been carried there by my sister, not with her fingers in position, but cradled in her arms like an infant.

When we were young, my sisters and I avoided baths, but we did not avoid the creek. In February, which was spring to us most years, we took off our shoes and waded across—about fifteen feet, knee-deep in water. When we emerged on the other side, it was as if the creek had given us warm, woolen socks, right up to the level the water had been. The cold was a lie; the river would hold us, keep our hearts beating. Our knees and our thighs shivered, but our shins and our feet—where the water had been—were like July.

We met the creek in every season. In one, it had spit up huge blocks of ice; we had to angle over them for miles. In another, we had to swing from tree to tree—or trunk to trunk—balancing on roots; the creek had tried to come and greet us. We put our mouths at the bottom of small cascades in feeder streams and drank it in. In every season, our feet were in it.

I am still a follower of creeks. On one of these walks, recently, I looked down and my shirt was covered with mayflies. The mayflies acted as if they were trying to lift me and take me away, like the picture of the four-and-twenty blackbirds carrying off the sheets the maid hung out to dry in the Mother Goose rhyme. I knew they were mayflies because of how they held their wings straight up when at rest—only mayflies and dragonflies cannot fold back their wings when not in flight—and because of how they curved their abdomens up away from the surface of my shirt in a barely noticeable puff of confidence. As I stared down at each of them, I could almost see the material of my shirt gathered in their tiny legs: six microscopic bunches of cotton per mayfly pulled up tight under each leg's single claw. Although they alighted on me and took flight again and again, they could not lift me up; I only kept moving forward, away from the stream, away from their home, the place where they were born, and would be born, through their children, again.

What I had experienced in miniature, on my walk along the small stream, happens en masse in other places. On certain evenings in late June or early July, along the shores of Lake Erie, you may not be able to walk at all. For there, in those weeks, huge numbers of mayflies metamorphose all at the same time, and the males swarm above the water. The females enter and choose a male, then leave with him to mate. But sometimes the swarms are blown inland by off water breezes. The mayflies are attracted to lights and accumulate at street corners in a fixed haze. When they die, piles of exoskeletons make the roads dangerously slippery for cars and passersby. The mayflies' crushed bodies must be swept up and carried away, like bagged autumn leaves, from sidewalks and porches. Some folks even suffer runny noses and scratchy throats, allergic to the husks of chitin invariably left behind after the clean-up of a misguided swarm.

The benefits of having mayflies, however, as any fisherman will tell you, far offset the occasional nuisance of a swarm. Fishermen have nicknamed adult mayflies "spinners," and if there is a swarm, most likely, there will be good fishing. Mayflies are preyed upon by trout, as well as by birds, minnows, water-striders, dragonflies, and frogs. Besides, most species of mayflies live, as adults, for only a few hours or a few days. Their lifespan at this stage is so short, in fact, that they do not even have working mouth-parts; there is no need to eat when there is so little time to complete the business of mating. So mayflies, as the insect order to which they belong—ephemeroptera—implies, are short-lived enough that a swarm is just bearable.

We were like most children, I think, my sisters and I, in our youthful hatred of taking baths. In summer the water would burn as we lowered our scratched bodies into the tub. It filled the signatures of the day's forays through fields and thorny hedges like dry creek beds, hotly flowing the length of our legs, which had finally cooled through dinner, at dusk; in those days, on our fine skin, even grass could cut. Sometimes, we were allowed to take what my parents termed a "bowl bath," during which we could stand on a towel by a sink filled with warm water and clean ourselves with a soapy washcloth. In this way, we could avoid that scintillating first dip into the tub.

During one of these, a bowl bath—and I must have been very young because I was not washing myself—I remember sitting on the bathroom counter facing my mother as she told me how in the olden days, this was the way they always bathed. She shared a room with her sister, and on their dresser sat a porcelain bowl full of water, which their mother would yell at them to change every day until finally, they did. Sometimes, in the morning, it would be covered with a thin layer of ice which they had to break if they wanted to wash their faces.

"I never rinsed," she said, as she rinsed me, "because the water was so cold." In the olden days, this is how it was.

It is obvious I had begun to put things in order: Adam and Eve, Columbus, my mother. But I'm not sure what kind of response I expected to my next question because I can't remember quite how old I was. Perhaps a date, a year, though the math would have been lost on me, would have been sufficient to fill the space of an answer. So far, time had consisted of only a past and a present, a past which began slightly before the birth of both of my parents, and a present that just was. So, could she tell me, please, when, exactly, the olden days were?

My mother's answer came as a shock. I had expected that the Olden Days was a period in history something like the Renaissance, or the Bronze Age, although surely I could not have known those labels then. Instead, I found that something I thought I had missed would be mine. Something I thought was before me was happening now, hadn't happened yet, and one day, wouldn't have happened for a long time.

"The olden days," my mother said, "are just a time that happened long ago. One day, you'll be telling your children about the olden days, too." She might as well have said, only the old get older; the young die. For that is nearly what happened that day: I began to remember, and lost a whole life.

Although it's true that individual adult mayflies may be short-lived, the order itself is a master of survival. Mayflies date from Carboniferous and Permian times—that's around 300 million years ago—and are the oldest winged insects still alive today. Most people's knowledge of mayflies stops short at their brief, bittersweet time as adults, those few hours or days when they are sexually mature but have only vestigial mouthparts, and are consumed by a frantic desire to reproduce. But young mayflies, called nymphs, can live in water for up to two years before completing their development. In other words, they spend the greater part of their lives as juveniles, overwintering in the tempered climate of the stream sometimes through two winters until, when they are large enough and it is warm enough, together, they become adults.

Every kindergartner learns about bugs. They bring home pictures of the monarch butterfly to color and, as the teachers suggest, they go over with their families the eternally inspiring stages of the butterfly's life: egg, larva, pupa, adult. The change from caterpillar to butterfly is so obvious that the metaphor of transformation is not lost even on them, as young as four and five. They add the impressively large word "chrysalis" to their vocabularies with pride.

But many insects, including mayflies, go through what is called "incomplete" metamorphosis, a life history which is skipped in many science classes, even at the high school level. These insects begin life as an egg, but then develop into a nymph, which is a creature that may or may not look like the adult. The job of the nymph is simply to get larger. It eats and molts, continuing to molt—sometimes up to 50 times, in the case of mayflies—until it is ready to transform into an adult. The major difference between complete and incomplete metamorphosis is that in the latter there is no non-feeding, immobile stage in which the larva spins a cocoon of some sort and waits through an often slow and extended transformation. Instead, an insect nymph simply molts one final time, unmasking—instantly, magically—the adult.

Many insects go through incomplete metamorphosis. This, in itself, is not unique. But when the mayfly nymph emerges from its final molt, it enters into a brief stage that is all its own. No insect order other than ephemeroptera enters into such a stage, called a subimago, or sub-adult. In this stage, the mayfly looks almost exactly like the adult, but is not sexually mature. The subimago, which still needs one more molt to produce a reproducing adult, actually has wings, unlike the nymph, and is capable of flight. The subimago lasts only, usually, for a few hours, just long enough to harden its new skin and then transform, shedding even a thin skin off its fragile wings, into the sexually mature adult.

The afternoon when I caught my sister washing her

trumpet, I had taken two steps from the hall, leaned forward, leaned back, and in those few seconds, seen transformed too many things: the trumpet as an organism, with valves refracted by water that bent from right to left as easily as arms and legs, and my sister as mother, bending over the tub; she would in fact be washing her own child when I was about as old as she was at the time. But perhaps what was most incredible of all was that in that room at that moment, in spite of the trumpet, there was no possibility of music.

It was as if she were momentarily frozen, dull, the dun, in the negative of some photograph that had not been developed yet, stuck in the flaps at the bottom of a box that had become this room. Her hair, pulled back so that it would not get wet, seemed to enlarge her eyes and place them on the sides of her head. She was looking out from herself, and I was looking in.

There she sat, perched on the side of the tub, no longer a flat character in the myth of my childhood. There was my sister, barely recognizable, hiding nothing. Her days of seeing things blurred by water were over, and she seemed to hesitate, knowing the transaction was already made. The trumpet, in its silence, was a traitor. Something had been cast off before both of us. She could fly, but she could not escape, for underneath there was something she must soon and silently orchestrate.

[2] *Too Ridiculous to Remember*

My grandmother did not live in Alabama, in a rotting plywood cabin at the foot of a mountain named Panther or Rattlesnake, her home equipped with a single, outdoor, cold-water spigot. On the contrary, she lived in a two-story farmhouse on a level acre just thirty minutes from the city of Baltimore, in the center of the village of Patapsco. She was surrounded on all sides by neighbors. Eventually, bright yellow aluminum siding replaced the stained cedar on the outside of the house, and new shingles sparkled on the roof. For Christmas she always put blinking, colored lights around the front door and on Halloween plastic pumpkins glowed in the upstairs windows. Her home had hot, running water in the kitchen. But somehow the upgrading over the years had not included putting in a bathroom. She was still using the chamber pot in the pantry or the outhouse at the corner of her property when I would visit her as a child in the late 1970's and early 1980's.

I don't remember ever using the outhouse or the chamber pot. I don't remember not using them either, although I know I must have neglected to at least once, when my mother was on a school field trip with one of my sisters, and I had been left at my grandmother's house. Nor do I remember finally letting go and wetting myself after what must have been hours of holding it in, or feeling wet, or mustering the courage to confess, or the trauma of being discovered. What I do remember is that, because there was no bathroom in the house, I was washed at the dining room table while seated on a cushioned chair. I had escaped the weirdness of peeing in the pantry, but then had to endure the oddity of taking a bath where I normally ate. My cousin, who was there too, was washed on a chair as well, as if my accident had also somehow tainted him. Maybe a bucket of water in that house was still too precious to waste on one child, and a clean child impossible to keep if a dirty one was around. Regardless, the two of us were soon straddling separate chairs, parked side by side as if on the wide seat of a bus. We were naked from the waist down, in this room where we usually shared Christmas dinner, eyeing a bucket full of soapy water set strangely on the patterned carpet, waiting for that shameless, efficient swipe of my grandmother's washcloth.

When the United States Census came out in 1940—the first time, I suppose, it asked about toilets—citizens were offered five choices: a) flush toilet in structure, exclusive use; b) flush toilet in structure, shared use; c) non-flush toilet in structure; d) outside toilet or privy; e) no toilet or privy. Forty years later, had my grandmother been asked this same question, she would have checked letter "d," having remained in the 2.5% of the population that still lacked an indoor toilet by that decade.

By the time I was five or six, my grandmother dropped out of that 2.5% and had a bathroom added on to her home. I was happy to use it, of course, every Christmas after dinner, or every January 2nd—my grandmother's birthday—after cake and ice cream, but in that second floor room, balanced on the toilet, staring out a large window that seemed new but had in fact always been there, I would experience a weird kind of vertigo. On the other side of the glass was the tip-top of a fir tree that grew very close to the house. I watched as the tree blew in the wind, and sensed that I was moving with it; all of a sudden I felt very flimsy and uncertain of the entire room, so recently built, the glue perhaps still wet or the boards too warped to hold the weight of a whole new space. I worried that the room might blow off the house entirely. Outside, I would check to see that the bathroom was not teetering off the edge of the first-floor roof. But try as I might, I could not find that room. There was the fir tree. There were the windows. But the shape of the house was unaltered, the same as it always had been. Where was the new room I had just come from, that had been added on to the house I knew? I was unable to fathom that a room could be divided, that a new room created within walls already there. Every time I entered the bathroom, sure enough, the mirror above the sink stared back at me. I could see myself in a room I could not see except when I was in it. It was as if the bathroom sprouted unaided from the second floor only when in use, as if the parts didn't mean anything, the sum always the same. I puzzled and puzzled, trying to fit in that extra room. Something had been altered inside my grandmother's home, an extra piece added, an entire era gone, but nothing on the outside appeared to have changed at all.

Because she was so practical—daughter of farmers, member of the women's society at church—a few things my grandmother did seemed so extravagant as to be out of character, like setting up the plastic Halloween pumpkins each year, and putting up the large-sized Christmas lights that outlined the front door, one side blinking awkwardly on and off while the other three sides shone continuously, pretending not to notice.

Also peculiar was the amount of food coloring she put in the bread-and-butter pickles made with cucumbers from her garden; it turned them a neon green so bright they looked toxic. On holidays she made ice cubes out of punch. And that is also when she brought out the root beer in large two or three gallon glass jugs, with their tiny handles and narrow pouring necks. Home-made, it never tasted quite right to our young mouths—my sisters, my cousins and me. It was a little too sweet and not carbonated, or, at least, not carbonated enough. But we drank it anyway, because we could see it was something the adults loved.

One year, as I sipped my root beer from a paper cup, something slipped into my mouth and onto the surface of my tongue. Although it did not move, I could tell it was alive. Somehow I spit it out without gagging and escaped upstairs to the bathroom with an older cousin. Leaning over the sink, we passed the root beer carefully from cup to cup until we had isolated the soft, undefined object in an empty one. It looked like a giant euglena with a root-beer colored eyespot. We ran downstairs to show our parents, who did not make their own root beer, but whom we trusted would know what it was: a bit of undissolved yeast, collected and clumped into the shape of something I had seen once in science class under a microscope. The memory of the euglena had changed its proportions in my mind, but I had sensed, rightly, that this thing was somehow alive.

Before my oldest sister, and even that oldest cousin, was born, my mother had a miscarriage at my grandmother's house. Because there was no bathroom, you can guess where it happened. I don't know the details: whether it was sudden or expected, if she was just visiting, or if she went there for help. This is from a conversation that my mother and I had when I was six or seven, and only once. She told me this while stirring the gravy we used to make out of tomato soup to pour over meatballs and white rice; I don't know how the subject came up. My grandmother put the older brother or sister (how could they not have known which? I wondered) into a canning jar and they rushed to the hospital, but it was too late—or too early. My grandmother canned many things and I knew this, but I always imagined the baby in a root beer jug—the only thing remotely large enough to fit an infant as I knew one. So there was my older brother or sister, like a ship in a bottle, squeezed through the thin neck of the jug, its room all window as they rushed to the hospital, and the whole world, instead of one tree, blowing interminably by it.

We first noticed something was wrong with my grandmother when she called to inform us that someone had stolen her cantaloupes.

"What?" my mother inquired, squinting, holding the

phone close.

"My cantaloupes! I had six of them, almost ready to pick, down along the corner of the garden farthest from the house. And this morning they're gone! All six of them!"

The first time, we hung up the phone and wondered— could someone have stolen the cantaloupes? Was someone in Patapsco angry at my grandmother over something? But then she called us back a few hours later and confided, laughingly, "They're still there. All six of them! Ripe and ready to be picked." Or maybe we drove to her house and took her out and stood at the corner of the garden to see for ourselves. Maybe my mother pointed down at each individual fruit, clinging to the vine, safe and ripe. "See? There they are, mom. They're still there. Why did you think they were gone?" Most probably, my grandmother simply didn't mention the incident the next time she called.

"Did you go out to look for your cantaloupes? Were they there?" we would have asked.

"What? Cantaloupes? Sure, I've got six of them out in the garden, just about ready to be picked."

"Do you remember that you thought someone had taken them?" we would prod. "Was it just that they were hidden? Had they rolled under something?"

"Huh? Who would want my cantaloupes?"

I don't remember which way it happened. All I know is that one moment her cantaloupes were gone, and a moment later they were back again, untouched, but something else was lost.

In spite of what our brains may know, it is difficult to react to anything other than what they perceive. When my grandmother was diagnosed with Alzheimer's disease, she was stripped of all her responsibilities: home, garden, cooking. In less than a year, we had moved her in with us. She must certainly have felt suspicious, if not of the disease, which we told her about but about which she seemed not to care, then of us—whom she still recognized at first but who had taken from her all of her work, her life.

Once, my mother was putting away cans of tomatoes she had just brought home from the grocery store. My grandmother stood watching nearby and suddenly snatched a can from my mother's hand.

"Those are my tomatoes!" she growled, accusingly.

"They are not," my mother rebuked, wrestling the can from her old mother's hand, and then banging it down on the shelf.

I know how my mother felt: wounded, like a child disciplined for something she hadn't done. We were appalled that my grandmother dare accuse us, her new providers, of taking something that was hers. Regardless of what we knew about her condition, we felt unfairly persecuted. In spite of what the doctors had told us, in spite of every article we had read about dementia, living with my grandmother during this time was like standing outside of her house so many years ago; we could not gain access to this new place in her mind. What was important to us at that moment— which really begged compassion or diversion—was our own reality: to make sure my grandmother understood that the can of tomatoes was ours and not hers, and that we would fight her for it.

Scientists at the University of Plymouth have successfully trained goldfish, popularly rumored to have just a three second memory span, to push a lever to get food at the same hour every day. First, they rewarded the goldfish for pushing the lever by giving them food. Then they reduced the reward to just one hour of the day. Eventually, the goldfish stopped randomly pushing the lever. When it approached feeding time, they began pushing the lever again and stopped at the end of the feeding hour whether food had been dispensed or not. They remembered this behavior for up to eleven months.

Gradually, before her diagnosis, we began to see that what was fast becoming lost was my grandmother's memory. Worried that she might forget to eat, we would ask her what she'd had for dinner. Once, she replied, "Three baked potatoes."

"Most people," we suggested, "will eat one baked potato . . . and a hamburger . . . and a vegetable, for example." But she would just nod her head and smile.

In addition to showing that the goldfish had memories exceeding my grandmother's near the end of her life, the researchers at Plymouth University had also proved that goldfish could tell time. This, too, began to escape my grandmother. And I can see now how it would be difficult to have one without the other—memory without time. For twenty years, every Friday morning at eight or eight-thirty, my mother had paused her car for a few moments on the precarious curve of road in front of my grandmother's house to pick her up for their weekly grocery shopping. But early one Monday or Tuesday morning, in the dark hours, a ringing phone woke my family up. I imagine my mother, breathless in the kitchen at two a.m., holding the receiver in shock.

"Well? Are you coming?" my grandmother's voice would

have sounded oddly calm.

"What? Where?" My mother's heart must have begun to beat with that middle-of-the-night phone call terror.

"Shopping! I'm just sitting here waiting."

We can't really know what happened that night in my grandmother's house. Was it something forgivable, forgettable? Did she stumble downstairs in a dream and dial our number? Or were the negatives that soon formed in our minds more correct: was she waiting at the dining room table all dressed, her pocket book sitting next to her with its expectant straps, listening for my mother's car? We could understand how at some point in life one might lose the whereabouts of a watch, or that a clock might become too complex, its Roman numerals like runes of some ancient text. But hadn't she opened the curtains to reveal the darkness outside, or at least noticed that behind them, drawn, the only light came from the moon? Or was her entire world, at that moment, that room?

After she moved in with us, I had to watch my mother take my grandmother apart each night, and in the morning attempt to put her back together again.

"Your teeth! Your teeth, mom!" my mother would say each evening before bed, pointing to my grandmother's mouth, trying to get her to take out her dentures. My grandmother would laugh in response. My mother would commence to tug at her own incisors, upper and lower, clacking her fingernails on their enamel, repeating her useless commands over and over, gesturing at a glass of water on the bathroom counter.

Perhaps at that point the world had become too ridiculous to remember. If teeth could be false then what were the words formed by them? I listened to my mother and grandmother in the bathroom together trying to pass the truth back and forth between them, the wrong one frustrated and the other one smiling, none of us able to create any meaning.

My grandmother did not live in Alabama. She lived on the East Branch of the Patapsco River. At the bottom of the hill just below her garden, a small spring emerged from the hillside and produced a tiny meandering stream that nearly lost itself in dry weather on the way to the river. But where it sprang from the hillside, the water was always clear and plentiful, and emerged with such force that one could easily collect a sample of it in midair before it completed its fall into the pool. For years my grandmother fought with the man next door over her property line, over whether it fell at the top of the hill, or at the bottom. They argued from their neighboring porches over who owned the spring as if they were pioneers settling the west. Even in this century, and this far east of the Mississippi, they remembered what is necessary for life.

There were creeks all around us, but whenever my sisters and I won a goldfish at the carnival, it was to this little spring—regardless of to whom it belonged—that my parents always brought us to collect water for the fishbowl. While my friends sat, heads-in-hands, at kitchen tables in their townhomes, their own goldfish swimming in small circles in the squat plastic bags we brought them home in, my sisters and I were down at my grandmother's house, straddling her spring. We didn't have to wait the suggested twenty-four hours for the chemicals to evaporate from a pitcher of tap-water. At my grandmother's house, in an instant we filled their bowls, gave them a room of water so transparent it was impossible to hide, impossible to forget, and I still remember: it was a room we could take home, and there was life inside it.

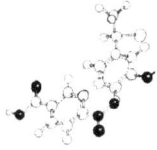

[3] *A Theory of Everything*

When I was a child, I could hear the sound of the earth turning. It was similar to the voiced exhale my mother would make as she got up from the floor after playing with us: louder than a sigh, a contented groan, as if whatever was overburdening was expected, satisfying. I knew, from age seven or eight, that the earth both rotated on its axis and revolved around the sun, so whenever the air would reverberate in my ears as a jet streaked through the sky above, I assumed it was just the earth moving herself along. Without looking up from my play to notice its true cause, I likened this occasional churning of atmosphere to the pushing of earth against sky as she flew through space. I believed that if I stood very still for very long, like the basketball net on its pole at the edge of our driveway, I would be able to feel myself turning with her, feel my place beyond earth's sky, as I faced a different corner of the universe.

My mother tried to explain that this was impossible, that everything would turn with me: the pole, the pavement, my parents' cars, the sky. Clearly, I was of this planet, locked to its journey so inescapably, anything I might try to use for reference was in the same small, tight frame as I. And shadows did not appease me; their indirect confirmation of the earth's daily journey around its axis was something I saw and understood listlessly, without much spirit. For at that age, all knowledge had to fit with my own experience. What I knew—what I was taught and what I read—must be provable by what I could perceive.

When I was a child, I could see molecules. They danced in rays of sunlight, while behind me my mother raced across all our surfaces with the torn sleeve of one of my father's old undershirts, trying to erase the cosmic dust from our house. At dusk, atoms quavered in the furniture. Before my half-open, slightly myopic eyes in the low light, my desk and bureau wavered like mirages while I tried to fall asleep, matter in constant flutter. And sleep, that effortfully-attained, heavy, unarouseable sleep of childhood, before the regular memory of dreams, was a wormhole. Like one of those theoretical passageways from a black hole to a white hole, from one time and place to another, sleep transported me from nighttime to morning with no more than the blink of an eye; I marveled at how time could pass every night without my experience of it.

Sometimes, though, I would wake prematurely, before morning, by a leg or a forearm that, deprived of blood from my lying on it for too long, was beginning to fall asleep itself. I would walk the hallway half-conscious, feeling not fully formed, at some earlier stage in evolution, my hands like the pincers of a lobster. Pincers at my sides, fingers melded together, I would try to tap my thumbs alive. Other times, I would wake up somewhere else entirely, and stare starkly from the darkness at our planet among nine. I couldn't imagine where I was then, and I couldn't imagine that sometimes I was not wherever I was at that time.

I'm not sure what to call this combination of precociousness and ignorance. Perhaps it should be called what it was—childhood. I must have been perceptive enough to understand the existence of two very nonhuman worlds: the one in the sky and the one in a molecule, as well as the fact that life on earth had adapted itself for billions of years before producing what I was. Someone must have thought me old enough or smart enough to teach about the motions of certain celestial bodies, about the behavior of the atoms in a kitchen table. And yet I had not picked up on the fact that this knowledge came to us not through our own ears and eyes, but through the use of complex technology, radio telescopes and electron microscopes, instruments that extended the capabilities of our five simple senses to proportions that evolution probably never could have surmised, and didn't need to, for what we tend to discover scientifically is nearly always curiously similar to what we already instinctively know.

Cosmologists are in pursuit of a theory of everything. Called the T.O.E., or sometimes the super unified theory, it would explain, in the simplest terms, everything from black holes to electrons. More specifically, a T.O.E. would reconcile the four fundamental forces under which we currently classify every interaction in the universe. These forces, listed here in the order in which they are most comprehensible to me, a non-physicist, and with only the simplest qualifiers, are gravity, the attraction between all objects with mass; electromagnetism, the attraction and repulsion of electrically charged particles, responsible for holding atoms and molecules together; the strong nuclear force, which holds together the nucleus of an atom with its equally charged (and thus repulsive) protons; and the weak nuclear force, which acts on quarks and leptons, the building blocks of protons, neutrons, and electrons, and is accountable for some types of radioactive decay.

Small steps have been made toward a T.O.E. In the 1960's, physicists showed that electromagnetism and the weak nuclear force are really two different manifestations of the same underlying interaction. They have labeled the union of these two fundamental forces the electroweak theory. Physicists are now trying to link electroweak theory with the strong nuclear force in what they call the grand unified theory. A grand unified theory has not yet been achieved but seems attainable since all three of the fundamental forces it aims to join deal with the physics of particles at or near the atomic level, also known as quantum mechanics. But long before even the electroweak theory, Albert Einstein began the search for a T.O.E. by spending most of his life trying to amalgamate electromagnetism and gravity. He did not succeed. We are still in search of a theory that will link Einstein's theory of general relativity, his geometric description of the weak but very long-ranged force of gravity, with quantum mechanics.

Notwithstanding the order in which I listed the four fundamental forces above, most of us are still trying to understand Einstein's conception of gravity. In elementary school, we jump off our chairs and give it a name. In high school, we drop balls of different sizes, study inclined planes, talk about forces, laws, acceleration. But to really understand gravity, we are on our own. And every year, every month, every week I must have it re-explained. Gravity is not some mysterious power that can reach across vast expanses of outer space. Gravity is something, something physical. It is a disturbance, a curve or a ripple in the actual fabric of space-time, caused by the mass of a planet, or an apple, or you or me.

The classic example in every science textbook is to think of space as a waterbed, and place a planet—a golf ball—upon it. A marble placed near the golf ball will travel toward the golf ball because of the depression in the surface of the waterbed caused by the golf ball's mass. That is gravity: the depression in the waterbed.

Or you could emerge from the forest like my oldest sister and I one day in early March. There are two ways to get to the creek, our destination, divided by a corridor of trees. The one on the right is long, with a gradual descent that requires walking through cut-up stalks of corn. The one on the left, a hayfield, drops abruptly to the river valley, barely plowable. On this day, at the top, sits a toboggan.

There are no farmers with children around here, no other houses. Although we do not own the land, these woods belong to us; we have made the paths with deer. The toboggan has appeared seemingly from nowhere, with no string to tow it there or away. It is old and wooden like we have never seen, just a few planks bound with metal and curved at the front end, long enough for several people. At first, I remember looking doubtfully around at ground mostly bare of snow. The thatch was webbed with blotches of white from a storm that probably got us no days off school and which we had long forgotten about. Like beached starfish, the unmelted patches of snow strewn across the field groped for one another, promising nothing. We would sooner pedal a bike than take out our sleds in conditions like this. Nonetheless, the toboggan at the top of the hill—our discovery, our experience—was like a textbook illustration for the potential energy available from gravity, and we understood it. In blind faith, we boarded; it took us to the bottom breathless and fast. With nowhere to go but the creek we went down, and could have gone farther, it seemed, let gravity pull us through the water and into the creek and into the center of the whole marvelous sphere but for rolling off at some undetermined but simultaneous moment and stopping by our knees and elbows and sneakers.

Raising ourselves from the ground, we continued on to the creek. I assume the toboggan was still there at the bottom when we returned and that we must have passed it by, too lazy to haul it to the top for another ride—remarkable though it was—knowing that would only mean trudging up the hill a second time after our descent. The toboggan at the top of the hill was a phenomenon we came across only once, although we walked that route many times. But it was enough to make us understand gravity and more—that as the sun tugged at the earth, something quite physical pulled us to the creek, and that if we stopped moving in our own circles, like the planets in our solar system—going to school, to church—we would be drawn there explicably.

Some cosmologists think we are on the verge of a T.O.E. It is called superstring theory. In superstring theory, everything in the universe is composed not of particles but of strings, which are really tiny, one-dimensional rips in the waterbed—the fabric of space-time. The rips can be open—like a straight line—or closed—like a loop—and their vibrations produce the charge and mass of the particles we know. Like the theory of general relativity—Einstein's theory of gravity—string theory does not describe forces, but properties of space, physical things. This is a significant similarity. Furthermore, one type of vibration of a closed string produces a particle with the exact characteristics scientists would expect of the particles which carry gravity, linking general relativity—gravity—to electromagnetism—the string's vibration. Superstring theory is the closest thing to a T.O.E. that modern physics can currently offer.

An interesting consequence of superstring theory is that it also predicts the existence of many more dimensions than the three we live in—mathematicians have calculated up to eleven so far, and believe there may be even more. These dimensions exist, apparently, all around us, less than a proton away, but are so compacted that we cannot sense them even with our finest instruments, which are unable to detect matter smaller than about a thousandth the size of an atomic nucleus. Physicist Brian Green, author of The Elegant Universe and The Fabric of the Cosmos, compares the extra dimensions to the circular loops of thread in the pile of a tightly woven carpet. At every point in the familiar world—the air in front of your face, the skin of your hand itself—these curled-up extra dimensions exist. They are also called degrees of freedom, because the more dimensions you have, the more you are free to do.

Freedom is not what my sisters and I needed in our youth, at least, not in regards to the universe. We did have rules—rules in the house, in school, in dealing with other people. But the woods and the hours belonged to us. We were free for the day in the forest. We drank from streams and ate our lunches on rocks. But when we were little, and came upon a forked tree in the woods, or two trees a shoulder's width apart, or a vine that opened at its base, or a bough that arced, we wondered if they were doors to another dimension.

Cautiously, my middle sister would put an arm or a leg through the passage in question, and I would peer to the left or right of whatever framed that particular door, to ascertain whether the limb was still in view. The theory was that if we could still see her hand or foot, passing through the door would keep us here on earth, in the same woods. If the limb became suddenly invisible, then the mass of vines and trees on the other side of the door was a hoax, and passing through would place us in what string theory has since mathematically predicted exists: some sort of parallel universe.

Any type of play could be interrupted by the discovery of a new portal; testing the possibility of a journey took precedence over all other games. I was horrified, however, on the day when I spoke out loud that I would not actually continue through a passage that turned out to be a true door and my sister responded, with confidence, that she indubitably would. I was so angry that I badgered her with questions. What if you weren't positive the door would be there for your return? But she wouldn't budge. What if you might never see your family again? It didn't matter. For whatever reason, she was insistent that if we ever lost sight of the limb she poked through a seeming threshold during one of our investigations she would follow that mystery through, step into an unseeable self, an unknowable world, an untraceable journey.

I did not believe her. I was so adamant that she would not actually do it that I tried to trick her by making what I thought would look like a true door to another universe. I spent an entire afternoon searching for a place in the forest to hang a large, rectangular piece of black cloth I had cut from an old Halloween costume. I fought with fishing line for an hour or more, trying to bind the cloth vertically by all four corners so it would billow in the wind loose and door-like.

She and I were really battling that day about the pull of family, our differing tolerance for risk, our inherent pessimism or optimism regarding what adventure might bring. But more important was our firm and shared belief, pre-string theory, that we could quite possibly stumble upon an opportunity to leave the recognizable world.

According to an article in the February 2004 issue of Discover magazine, physicists whose theories do not turn out to be wrong at least 50 percent of the time are not creative enough. Paul Steinhardt and Neil Turok, cosmologists at Princeton and Cambridge Universities, by mastering the equations of superstring theory, are gambling with none other than a new theory of the origin of the universe.

In Steinhardt's and Turok's view, our universe did not start with a small, dense, extremely hot big bang. Instead, it started out cool and vacuous, as a greatly expanded universe which existed on a three-dimensional sheet, called a membrane, or "brane," made up of stretched strings. This sheet was suspended in the higher—and invisible—dimensions of the cosmos, curiously like the cut-up witch's cloak I envisioned hanging in our forest. All around us hung other universes on their own sheets. Occasionally, after a trillion or so years of expansion, the forces between two sheets would cause the sheets to ripple and collide, with the peaks of their ripples hitting first and then the valleys, much as the wind might billow your laundry together when you have hung it out to dry.

This type of uneven collision, say Steinhardt and Turok, produces a universe that looks remarkably like the one in which we live, with its cold and hot spots, clusters of galaxies separated by empty voids, and accelerating expansion. The traditional inflationary big bang model also predicts our current situation. The difference is in what happens next: in the traditional model, time, which had a beginning with the big bang, will one day end. There is no way around it. According to the more recent, colliding branes theory—dubbed ekpyrosis—branes collide again and again, recreating universe after universe. Time has no beginning or end, just birth, destruction, and rebirth. This is a more appealing theory, the article notes, for even the most secular physicist to stomach.

For a while as a child I had my own T.O.E.: whatever I wanted to happen didn't. I remember walking down our driveway to wait for the school bus hoping to fail a social studies test, sitting in the chair at the haircutter's wishing my haircut would turn out horrible. Saying over and over in my mind, so the cosmic ears could hear it clearly, and then turn things around: I don't want a chemistry set for Christmas. This inner reverse psychology worked for a while; with little conscious hope of anything my expectations of how things would turn out were nearly always met or surpassed. But gradually what I had to wish for would become too horrible to say: I hope a certain boy hates me. I hope my dad does not get a job. I hope my grandfather dies from this brain tumor. So I would turn to some newer theory, something more tolerable, and the tics and habits of youth became like superpowers. Blinking hard or cracking my knuckles in a certain order could command the universe.

And when they didn't, when things did not seem to go as predicted, like those nights when I would wake not fully formed, I was easily reborn. My mother would lead me back to my room, untwist my sheets and make the bed over me, like mothers do everywhere for children who have wet themselves, or had nightmares, or have worries, bringing down cool pockets of air over our hot, confused bodies. The smooth surface of the sheet comes to rest first on the toes, knees, and hips, and then on the dips in between. And as quickly as that, we know who, what, and where we are.

Recently, I spent some time with my newest niece. She is not quite two, and we didn't so much play together as hang out with each other for a few hours in my parents' basement. Amid the clutter of colorful plastic toys, she scampered around and picked up nearly anything she could to throw and watch fall. It is her newest joy, this game the earth plays with her, consistently bringing down anything she erratically raises from its surface.

At one point, a wash of light fell upon her cheeks and chin as she stepped into the path it was taking through a narrow upper window. She stopped and laughed, throwing back her head and shoulders so the light, the heat, moved down to her neck. Mesmerized, she stepped repeatedly into and out of it, waving her arms one moment, then laughing the next, and I realized she was in touch with what I had once been in touch with, tiny particles that danced in the lighted air to the rhythms of her moving hands. Precociously—mistakenly—I had called them molecules, correlating what I knew with what I had experienced.

Even today, when I hear a plane or a jet overhead I cannot shake that first impression. It still feels like the friction of earth against sky, reminding me of earth's journey. At some point, what sends us searching, in spite of all the things we find out, only brings our return. Myth and fact, equally satisfying, are quite possibly no different. We have put ourselves on the map and stretched the map as far as the entire universe, and now, whatever its architecture, we must learn to call that universe home. Like a child, I am ready for anything: big bangs, colliding branes, for what we see now—and I would be loath to give that knowledge up—I knew already early on and I know others did too: if you blink one eye and then the other, rap your left knee twice and then the right one, the world will stay in order. And if you're sure to pause and touch a certain stone each day on your way home from school, the world will be beautiful.

[4] Weeds Together

We were plant people: my mother and father, my sisters and I. I don't mean to say that we were vegetarians, or crop farmers, or even that we ever had a garden, but that we were drawn to the outside because of what grew there, and not because of what moved and hid, what we might occasionally find or glimpse. We opened our doors to what we knew would boldly and effortlessly be there each day, and seemingly had been always: a valley, a ridge, the trees, and the river. We loved the borders of life, and not the living.

Of course we had pets: fish, a dog, parakeets, hermit crabs. We kept the occasional turtle which strolled through our yard in a box on the porch for a few hours. Daily my mother filled a birdbath with water, and once a couple of northern orioles made their hanging nest at the top of the tree that marked second base for our wiffle-ball games. But we never actively turned over rocks or logs looking for salamanders or snails, like I read about in the biographies of the naturalists I love. We rarely followed tracks in the snow. We seldom fished long enough to catch anything, and not once

45

with worms. Mostly, animals were something we endured, like mosquitoes, and the occasional case of chiggers. We cowered from the sounds of owls and neighbors' cats at night. Our feelings were only legitimized by the pileated wood-pecker that startled us one Saturday morning. It landed on the base of a maple tree outside my sister's window that we were surveying as we planned our day. For an instant, we took in its profile; it stared at us oddly with one eye, its bright colors and sharp angles an alarming testament that almost anything might be lurking in our forest.

At that time, we used only our physical senses to determine what was benign. I did not know this then, but the pileated woodpecker was a healthy native to our shared landscape. In spite of its elusiveness, and its jarring, cartoon-ish look when it did appear within our view of the forest framed by a bedroom window, that woodpecker belonged in the terrain of my childhood. What did not belong we were sometimes fully conscious of and hated: an epizootic virus, gypsy moths. But just as often we were ignorantly enamored with our invaders—for instance, some of the plant species that touched our shoulders and knees as we explored the forest we loved, a place we thought they—and we—could truthfully call home.

It could have been the rabies scare in the Mid-Atlantic states in the 1980's that made us, always lovers of habitat, ultimately wary of inhabitants. During that time, we were duly skittish about animals which we knew were carriers of the disease; raccoon tracks on a muddy shore we waded over to were enough to keep us away from a favorite section of creek for a day or more. But our wariness back then grew to exceeding proportions. I remember trembling in the basement while my mother dialed the county health department one December. My dog had been poking around the remains of a dead deer in a snowy field. Then she licked my sister on the mouth. I was putting on my winter clothes again to take my father to the place where the deer lay. I pulled them down from the line where they hung next to my sister's empty, dripping ones while she sat upstairs in a chair, waiting for her sentence. "Why would you let her lick you after that?" my mother asked, exasperated and worried. My sister couldn't answer. No matter that deer, as herbivores, rarely contract rabies, which is spread by infected saliva. We were terrified enough as a family to spring into action: my mother calling for a second opinion, my father going out to examine the evidence first-hand. But the dead deer turned out to be a roll of brown carpet, a discarded scrap that looked like a flap of torso tucked into the snow from where we had eyed it cautiously while sledding. My father kicked it with his boot and shook his head, revealing the synthetic rubber underneath, unraveling for an instant the irrationality of our fear.

My father was the only one in our family—if there was one—who, as the man of the house, did not harbor the unfounded apprehension of wild animals that the rest of us had. Still, I have seen him more than once lose his cool, dancing halfway across the yard to flee the threat of a honeybee.

In 2007, The Congressional Research Service produced a report for Congress on this little critter, titled Recent Honeybee Colony Declines. The report gives due credit to the honeybee for its noble role in producing about 1/3 of the food products in the U.S. diet, attributing to it a long list of fruits, nuts, vegetables, and clothing fibers. According to the report, the honeybee is responsible for 90-100% of the pollination of almonds, apples, avocados, blueberries, cherries, cranberries, kiwi fruit, macadamia nuts, asparagus, broccoli, carrots, cauliflower, celery, cucumbers, onions, legume seeds, pumpkins, squash, and sunflowers. Honeybees are partially responsible, the report goes on to say, for the pollination of yet another long list of plant foods: apricots; citrus fruits such as oranges, lemons, limes, grapefruits, and tangerines; peaches; pears; nectarines; plums; grapes; brambleberries; strawberries; olives; melons such as cantaloupe, watermelon, and honeydew; peanuts; cotton; soybeans; and sugar beets.

But in October of 2006, beekeepers along the East Coast began noticing sudden, higher-than normal, declines in their honeybee populations. By the end of the year, beekeepers on the West Coast were reporting similar severe losses. In the winter of 2006-2007, according to the Apiary Inspectors of America and the USDA-ARS Beltsville honeybee Lab, there was a 31.8% loss of bee colonies in the U.S. This loss increased slightly to 35.8% in the winter of 2007-2008. Last winter, the loss decreased to just 20%. This is still, however, an alarming number, amounting to 1/5 of the estimated 2.3 million United States bee colonies. But what is almost as troublesome as the quantity of bee colonies lost, is the fact that the bees seem to be just disappearing. Beekeepers are simply opening their formerly crowded hives to find only an egg-laying queen, her brood, and a few workers. There are no dead bees inside the hive, nor are there dead bees lying outside of it, near the entrance, where workers whose job it is to keep the hive clean will carry a bee whose life has ended. So curious is the mystery of the missing bees that some scientists have sardonically suggested the bees are being abducted by aliens. Without much initial evidence as to the root of the problem, this unsettling phenomenon has been dubbed Colony Collapse Disorder.

When she was a child, and even now, my mother has told me, her nightmares often consist of being chased by large, wild animals. "Don't you ever dream there is a bear charging behind you," she has asked, "and your feet just can't move fast enough, or the door you are leaning against might give in?" I haven't; my own bad dreams are always of climbing vertically inclined hills by pulling myself from tuft of grass to tuft of grass. The fear is that the roots might not hold.

Nonetheless, my mother always shared her personal night terrors with my sisters and me at the breakfast table. And by age nine, scenes from Old Yeller were already embedded in our heads. On top of this, everyone half-believed that the treatment for rabies still consisted of a long series of painful shots in the stomach. The resulting mindset led us to regard every raccoon, and nearly every other animal that we saw, with the same prejudice. If it were drinking from the creek, if the dog scared it up a tree in the daytime, if it slunk across the driveway in front of our car as we pulled in late at night, one of us would always offer up the following suggestion: "It might be rabid."

But nothing could keep us out of the forest, out of the creek, off of the rocks that banked it or the ice that formed there after three consecutive days of below freezing weather each winter. We would pause on a cold day, half-way to the creek, and turn our ears toward what we could not see yet through the trees, listening for the rush of water, hoping for the silence that meant the creek had frozen, that we had a new path on which to walk and explore our forest.

I like to think we had an instinctual knowledge that the rabies virus was a trespasser, something only recently introduced into our environment, thus validating our suspicion of any animal that might be associated with it. The first case of raccoon rabies in the U.S. occurred in Florida half a century ago. Had the disease been allowed to spread slowly and predictably on its own, the way it did throughout Florida and Georgia in the 1950's and 1960's, perhaps we would not have been so ridiculously afraid of infection. But in 1977, just two years after I was born, along the border of Virginia and West Virginia, the disease suddenly sprang up in an alarming number of wild animals. The reason is not a mystery: man hosted a rabies virus dinner party. In the 1970's, over 3,500 raccoons were taken from the southeastern states and relocated to Virginia and West Virginia to train coonhounds for recreational hunting. At least a few of the translocated animals were infected with rabies before they were moved. Upon relocation, these animals survived only long enough to pass on this new invader to their extremely less resistant cousins. The result: an epizootic, or epidemic of disease in the animal population, and humans who were extremely cagey about their wild neighbors.

Two other tiny invaders, it turns out, are now making their way around the United States—the tracheal mite, and the varroa mite. This time the victim is not mammals, but the honeybee. Both mites have been implicated as one of many factors of Colony Collapse Disorder. The first report of the existence of the tracheal mite came from the Isle of Wight in the English Channel in 1921. It was detected in the United States in Texas in 1984. The varroa, or vampire, mite, originally from Singapore, had moved into Hong Kong and the Philippines by the 1960's. In 1979, the varroa mite was found in Maryland, and had been reported in Wisconsin and Florida by 1987. It is not known just how either mite was introduced into the United States.

The tracheal mite, a microscopic, whitish, oval-shaped mite, spends its entire life cycle in the breathing tubes or air sacs of the adult honeybee. It attaches itself to the tracheal wall and sucks the bee's blood, then reproduces. Pregnant females leave their hosts through the spiracles—or breathing holes—in the bee's thorax, climb to the tip of a hair, then pass to another bee, where they enter again through the spiracles, travel into the breathing tubes, and lay their eggs. Individual honeybees heavily infested with tracheal mites are suffocated, and in their shortened lives, often are unable to fly.

Varroa mites are brown, crab-shaped, and, though larger than the tracheal mite, still less than 2 mm long and wide. Young mites feed on developing honeybee larva. They burrow their convex bodies into the larva's abdominal folds. Males and females mate in the cell, males die, and females emerge with the larva, where they then look for another cell with a developing larva inside on which to lay their eggs. Honeybee colonies infested with varroa mites usually exhibit dead young bees with malformed wings, legs, abdomens, and thoraxes near the entrances to their hives. But in Colony Collapse Disorder, remember, there simply are no dead bees, so tracheal and varroa mites can't be the only cause. Other factors might include additional parasites, viruses, pesticides, the stress of migratory beekeeping (the moving of colonies leased to agricultural producers on flatbed trucks from place to place during a single season) and even cell phone use, which has been shown to cause short and long-term memory loss in bees, preventing those out foraging for pollen from being able to make it back to their homes again.

Although we were plant people, when we were young, my sisters and I were not conservationists of the plants we loved by any means. We cut birch branches and saplings to make bows and used the tough, light stalks of sensitive fern for arrows. We picked pokeberries and mashed them in buckets, using brushes from our watercolor kits to paint rocks purple at random throughout the forest. We gathered acorns from the ground and hauled them back up to the tops of the trees, hording them in burlap sacks we had nailed mercilessly across the branches, and then took turns trying to pelt each other with them as we rode our dirt bikes in circles underneath. We were wilder than I can imagine; every day, at dinner, my mother would say, "Grandmom called and said she saw some monkeys in our trees."

Another creature I abhorred in my youth, like bats and raccoons—anything that could potentially carry rabies—was the gypsy moth. A little research shows that Maryland experienced the highest number of acres of forest defoliation from gypsy moths in 1995, but I know that they actually invaded my parents' three and half acres much sooner. This probably occurred in 1987, the summer I watched helplessly as a chunk of our forest, our foundation, our pride as plant-lovers, became completely stripped of its leaves.

The gypsy moth is native to Europe and Asia, and like the rabies virus, whose natural movement was sped up by the movement of humans, was brought to Medford, Massachusetts in 1869 by a man interested in mating the moths with silkworms to produce a disease-resistant species for commercial silk production. A few of the moths escaped, and their hardiness helped them to populate, and then defoliate, our native forests. In this country, gypsy moths are known as an invasive species, a non-native species that can out-compete native species in the native species' own environment, due to factors such as high reproductive rates in the exotic species, and a lack of natural predators, among other things.

At first I tried to ignore these new denizens, but a friend from school was disgusted; we went outside to play the morning after a sleepover but were stopped by larva that fell from the trees onto our shoes and shoulders. Our house was covered in caterpillars. The adult moths laid their foamy clusters of eggs in the protected grooves of the siding, as well as everywhere else: on our bikes, our skateboards. It was obvious, by their sheer numbers, that something was happening, that something was wrong. Powerless, we watched them defoliate our forest, which left us angry and exposed. When the adults had mated and gone, a next-door neighbor diligently moved from tree trunk to tree trunk with a coffee can of gasoline, scraping the masses into it, even though we knew each individual cluster, including the ones we couldn't reach, contained thousands of eggs.

We read that sometimes young, healthy trees could make a comeback after one year of defoliation, so every night

I prayed, because I believed in science and in God. I figured that if something or someone could make one thing happen for me, this might be it. It seemed like an unselfish wish. I deemed that my woods was supposed to exist, because for as long as I had been there, it had too. But after that summer there was a gap in our forest. The gypsy moths left the ash and black locust, but all the oaks were gone.

Understandably, there is great concern over Colony Collapse Disorder. Honeybees are so crucial to the almond industry in California that in spring, honeybee colonies are transported by truck from orchard to orchard, where bee-keepers stop periodically to ensure pollination of the crop. If the honeybee were wiped out, the worst-case scenario would be massive starvation; at the very least, there would be major changes in agriculture and the economy.

But what most people forget is that, like the rabies virus that held our reason hostage and the gypsy moths that decimated the oak trees in my family's forest, honeybees are not native to North or South America. Honeybees are not being abducted by aliens. Honeybees are aliens, at least to this continent. Before them, all of the pollination in the Americas was done by our own native bees: carpenter bees, bumblebees, sweat bees, and about 3,500 other species of mostly solitary bees. And the major crop that supported the inhabitants of the Americas before the arrival of the honeybee—corn—did not require bees to ripen; corn is pol-linated by wind.

Honeybees were first brought to Jamestown in 1616 to add sugar to the colonists' diet, as well as to pollinate the European plants the settlers had brought with them. Once such plant was white clover, which, as a grazing plant, was necessary for the livestock the colonists also introduced. The alpaca—an animal native to South America—was the only animal that had been domesticated on this continent prior to the arrival of the colonists.

The current U.S. agricultural economy has been based in large part on crops brought to America, such as wheat. Early on, the colonists saw that the smaller populations of solitary native pollen bees would not be capable of supporting vast monocultures of exotic plants. Honeybees, with single hives of up to 70,000 bees, were necessary neighbors for the settlers of this country. And so they were brought over intentionally, and with gusto, to do this essential work.

Raccoons frothing at the mouth, hanging out in yards at noon, or trees stripped of their leaves in a single season, because they are quite immediately visible, pull at our heart-strings. But the honeybee invasion, though far from acci-dental, has not been without its own negative effects. You just have to look a little harder for them. For instance, it has been argued that honeybees out-compete native bees (and birds) because they can more rapidly harvest nectar due to sharper abilities of detection and communication of nectar sources. Importing the honeybee may have resulted in declines in native bee populations. Furthermore, studies in Colorado have shown that although honeybees do pollinate species native to this continent, they prefer to pollinate exotic species. This suggests that the presence of honeybees may help speed up invasion of exotic plants by promoting the reproduction of invasive plants that native bees normally wouldn't visit. And finally, honeybees don't "buzz" pollinate, which is required by some of our native plants, such as tomatoes, and anything else in the nightshade family. Buzz pollination is achieved by hugging a flower-head and mechanically shaking the pollen out. Bumblebees, which are native, are most easily observed doing this. More alarming than the fact that honeybees simply don't do it, however, is that honeybees have been observed robbing pollen lodged in the stigmas of plants that have already been buzz-pollinated by native bees. Because honeybees support our food base, however, they are not technically considered invasive.

The invasive species problem, caused by humans moving things around on the planet in time periods far too short for natural selection to keep track of in the balanced way in which we normally like to think of nature, goes much deeper, and is much more complex than most of us would like to imagine. Even the simple earthworm, I am astonished to learn now, is an invader. Lauded by gardeners, farmers, and naturalists for aerating the soil, and re-releasing nutrients into the food chain, this seemingly harmless little inhabitant is a trespasser, and is leaving a mess of change in its wake. During the last period of glaciation, native earthworms in the Americas migrated south and left the northernmost areas relatively earthworm-free for about ten thousand years until humans stepped in once again. Colonists brought European and Asian earthworm species over with them in the rootballs of plants and in ship ballast. By quickly decomposing decaying matter on the forest floor, these invasive earthworms changed the chemistry of the soil in the entire northern half of North America. This, like the work of the honeybee, has made it easier for non-native plants to overtake native ones. It has also, by using up their food source, reduced the numbers of tiny insects and arthropods that were once this area's only decomposers. And the arthropods, in turn, can now barely support North America's unique salamander population. But since they arrived with us—because of us—like honeybees, earthworms don't look or feel like invaders.

My mother swears, swears she saw an armadillo cross the road in front of her by my childhood home in Maryland. And when I do a little research, I find that it is possible. Sure enough, she sends me an article a year or so later from the local newspaper describing how armadillos, escaped from zoos or abandoned as pets, can often survive far outside their normal range.

When I look back on the things we feared as kids, the things we thought were not supposed to be there, in our lives, I find they don't fit much with scientific reason. And many of the plants we loved have turned out to be invaders or, at least, non-native. We spent hours in summer snapping off the calyx of each carefully picked honeysuckle flower, slowly pulling the stamen backwards through the corolla, and then licking the drop of nectar that this delightfully produced. But it was Japanese honeysuckle we played with, introduced in the 1800's from Asia. As we visited flower after flower, sucking each one's tiny, perceived gift, we didn't notice—or care—that the dense bushes and mats the plant formed had smothered all the other vegetation in its path, that the vines had girdled and killed young trees as the plant climbed to reach the light. It was there when we were born, and so, like ourselves, we assumed that it belonged.

We made elaborate bouquets of oxeye daisy, and common wintercress, and chicory—all from Europe—and glorified in their abundance. Of course, I have learned now to hate Lady's Thumb and garlic mustard and to miss what it's replaced—natives like cut-leaved toothwort—but is this really fair? If I am going to be selfless enough to hate them, in mercy to our native species, shouldn't I also be selfless enough to despise earthworms and honeybees, despite the services they provide me? I understand that invasive species threaten diversity, but so, too, does mass agriculture. Who defines the borders, other than the species themselves, within which a certain species can live? The undeniable fact is, in my love of plants, many non-natives, like the Japanese barberry bush we hollowed out to make a cage for some game, were my playmates. I grew up with them, and they with me. We were weeds together. We are all invaders. For how long must we stay in one place to be considered native? My ancestors came across two continents to this one: from Africa, to Europe, to America. And with them, because of them, came all kinds of plants and animals, and the illogic of where we feel we belong and what we choose to love and hate.

PART II

Nymph

[5] Watch the Cord

For years, my mother ironed in a doorway. With each week's laundry, she stood at the juncture of two rooms—kitchen and living room—which comprised the west end of our small ranch-style home. Behind her, a short hall extended from the living room to three small bedrooms and one bathroom. I suppose it was convenient; to her right was the hall closet in which she kept the iron and board. She hung my father's collared shirts on hangers and rested them on the closet's doorknob before moving them all at once to the bedroom. This set-up also allowed my mother to watch television while she worked. But it was somewhat risky: the end of the board where the iron waited sat firmly anchored on the kitchen tile, where the iron's plug could reach an outlet; the rest of the board teetered, on the living room carpet, half an inch higher.

My sisters and I tried to reduce the traffic as much as possible during these times, but it was difficult to subdue our play, and the place where my mother stood provided access to many things: the basement, the outdoors. My mother would continually pause, look down, and warn, "Watch the cord!" as we slipped through the sleeve of space from the hallway to the kitchen for a pair of scissors, or a drink, and back again. We sensed our movement was unwelcome, but also that she wouldn't stop us; she only steadied the iron on the board, then looked down to supervise our inevitable leap over the cord.

It was quite the opposite of the favorite English folktale my mother sometimes read to us at night, about the woman whose pig wouldn't jump over the stile. We went willingly, didn't need a string of cause and effect, like the pig in the story, to get us to do something. Cat! Cat! Kill rat; rat won't gnaw rope; rope won't hang butcher; butcher won't kill ox; ox won't drink water; water won't quench fire; fire won't burn stick; stick won't beat dog; dog won't bite pig; piggy won't jump over the stile; and I sha'n't get home to-night. Unlike the pig, my sisters and I took this small step with haste, of our own accord. We didn't understand what could happen, what the story tried to teach, what my mother worried about: how one thing can lead to another. It would have been a disaster if the iron had fallen, if the cord had tripped one of us and the hot metal hit our backs. But it never happened.

Even in our own rooms, behind closed doors, we took these small, necessary steps, creating games that broke unspoken rules and ignored boundaries, in order to explore. In the evenings, sometimes one, or two, or the three of us would kneel on the pillow of my middle sister's twin bed in the room the two of them shared. We would open a window to new-fallen snow, secretly, quietly, so as not to summon our mother who would chide us for heating the entire forest. Our forearms rested, reverent, on the wet sill as they did on the communion rail at church. Inside, the house was immediate, warm, and responsive—the electric heat clicked on to replace whatever was lost through the open window, keeping the room a stable temperature. Outside was cold and new. It waited to see what we would do.

In our hands we held a special, homemade kind of toy: a key tied to a long piece of yellow yarn. It was an old house key, most certainly to a lock in a door that no longer existed; otherwise, we would not have been given the key to play with. Taking turns, we would throw the key out the open window, careful not to let go of the string. Phht. The key would hit the snow. Thht. We would draw it back again. Over and over we tossed the key and drew it in, as if this tool forged for the interior could also somehow give access to the forest, to snow we could not go out and play in until morning.

We did not talk. It seems as if we did not plan to play this, did not create the game together; one of us must have caught another playing, or were caught, and only then we began performing the ritual as a group of three. By morning, the strange tracks of the pulled key were always left unopenable, locked under late snowfall. The tracks were made by us, but by a body—a capability, at least—we did not yet recognize. I imagine that in between these games, the key lay bound on the surface of one of our bureaus, cocooned in its length of yellow yarn.

At the time, the game seemed mostly deceitful. We did not know the meaning. Now the message is more clear. It was a form of travel, of meeting with a different time and place than what the order in our house contained. When the key came back, it carried with it something just fallen, that melted over our room-warmed fingers, something that might have become old by morning. Touching the snow the evening before our mother announced schools had closed due to inclement weather, and we had been sanctioned a day to play in it, was an action we allowed ourselves, an action we intuitively felt we deserved. And, probably, no matter how aggravated my mother would have been had she found us with the window open in winter, no matter how ashamed we would have been at realizing we'd dragged water onto the bedspread and carpet—all those unanticipated consequences—it was an action we could not have prevented.

We are all changelings. Or, at least, something other than what our parents suspect us to be. If not from anything else, this is from the mere fact that our expectations of our parents are incongruent with their expectations of us. We must survive; they will die. It's not that children are ungrateful; it's just that all they must do to be loved is eat, drink, grow, and later, learn. But the parent must feed, clothe, hold, and for a lifetime, worry.

It wasn't until after its extinction from the U.K. in 1979 that scientists realized Britain's large blue butterfly, *Maculinea arion*, was a changeling with very specific parental needs. The pregnant female large blue would lay just one egg per flower bud of wild thyme. When the egg hatched, the flower and seeds of the wild thyme would serve as food for the caterpillar for two or three weeks. Then, after its last molt, the larva would drop to the ground and begin to secrete a sugary substance from a special organ near the rear of its body. The sugary substance would inevitably attract a red ant which, possibly believing the large blue was one of its own escaped ant larvae, would unwittingly provide the rest of the large blue caterpillar's nourishment.

The worker ant would carry the caterpillar into the ant nest where, over the span of eleven months, it would feed on ant eggs and grubs, hibernate, resume feeding, and pupate. Then, after nearly a year, the large blue would emerge from the interior of the ant nest and spread its broad, scaly wings.

How could the ant not perceive the changeling baby, plainly changing for all those months into a literal butterfly, and at the expense of its own children? And when do our parents perceive this of us? For from the time we are born, we are growing away from them.

Just east of our house, just over our property line, farther than the key on its string could reach, but still visible from my sister's window, was an old barn where we were not supposed to play. Nailing fallen rotten boards back onto their rotting supports, we built, inside it, a tree-house of sorts with the two boys who lived next door. Once, sliding down from one board to another, I scraped my knee and shin. We knew the wound should be cleaned, but also that it wasn't severe—it was from wood, not old metal, and wouldn't require a tetanus shot like when my sister had stepped on a nail. My mother had stepped on a nail, too, as a child. For both of them the nail went up through the sole of the shoe and into the foot. For a while I thought it was a rite of passage and was only waiting for my turn: first my mother, then my oldest sister, next my middle sister and finally me. But what I had, on that day, was basically a skinned knee.

Because we knew it wasn't severe, my oldest sister fashioned a lie for me to exchange for some peroxide and a band-aid. I carried that lie home with pride and certainty. Just a few yards from the barn, back on our own property, we sat on a fallen birch above a rock and acted out what might have happened. This time, even though we were using words to construct reality, unlike the game with the key, it did not feel devious. It didn't matter what had happened, just that what could have happened was as believable as what did; one thing needed to lead convincingly to the next. Perhaps what had happened didn't matter to my mother either, or what we said. Surely she could hear the pounding of the boys' blue-headed, squat-handled hammers from such a short distance away; she must have known we were with them, and that a wound was inevitable.

Farther than the barn, to the north, was a creek—which we always called a crick—from which coming home wet eventually became a habit. This was despite the gentle threats my mother would deliver as we left. We would pass her, standing with hands raised, at the entrance to the forest, hanging our laundered clothes on lines attached to poles made wobbly by our swinging from them, although we'd been told not to. She'd remove a clothespin from her mouth and warn us to stay out of the water. Sometimes we accidentally fell in. Often we splashed each other until we were so wet we could sit on the bottom of the creek and still come home and say we'd only been splashing, without sounding insincere. We thought it was just more laundry she wanted to avoid. We did not believe that it might be possible to drown in a small amount of water—a shallow creek, a bathtub, a bucket—simply because your mother wasn't looking.

My father built us a table in the woods, one leg of

which was a tree. He built us the table to give us some lift as we swung on a strong vine that hung in the middle of a clearing. Perhaps because of its pendulous motion, which always brought us back to our beginning—or, if we hung on for more than two swings, always gradually decreased in distance, dropping us in the dead center of the clearing—my father was able to allow us this journey.

But at this table, from my sister, came one sacred dare: to swing naked. I remember the wind on my whole skin and the peeling layers of vine I wrapped around as the vine had wrapped around its supporting tree. This was prehistoric, and prehistory was something I wasn't even sure my parents believed in. For this, from my sister, I received a fistful of coins—my own money, unlike the change I was given by my parents to buy specific things: a penny for the gumball machine. All of this was done undercover, with a strange mixture of fear and self-righteousness, feeling, I shouldn't but also I must.

Sadly, our love for our parents can never be as strong as their love for us. In the animal world, the energy parents expend on childrearing, even in something as inhuman as a fish, sometimes seems extraordinary. In South America, there are fish that lay their eggs out of water. Glued to leaves on low overhanging branches the fish have jumped from the water to spawn upon, their eggs are safe from predators. But the effort does not end there; regularly, the fish splash water up at the eggs to prevent them from drying out.

Sometimes the transfer of energy from parent to child is so direct, fatalities occur. During egg laying and incubation in eider ducks, females can lose up to 45% of their body weight. What's more, there are as many adult female deaths during the two-month breeding season as in the entire rest of the year.

Fecundity and adult survival are negatively correlated in a variety of species. Female house martins that raise two consecutive broods in one summer are more likely to die the following winter than females that raise just one. In an odd but reasonable twist, when fruit flies are denied mating, both males and females live longer. Although not all studies concur, the law of natural selection would predict competition within the individual between reproduction and survival, since what it selects for is fitness—which science defines as "reproductive success"—and not necessarily longevity of life.

One scientist, William Clark, believes that the phenomenon of death is itself a consequence of the evolution of sexual reproduction, without which, of course, there would be no such thing as "parents." In other words, once parents came along, so did death. By loading resources into reproductive cells, somatic—or body—cells, such as those which operate in your liver or your heart, are subject to senescence, rather than repair, and are, ultimately, sacrificed when the individual dies. Although Clark's theory is built on cells, the sacrifices parents make are often all too evident: in some species of mites, the young develop all the way to sexual maturity inside the body of the mother. Brothers and sisters mate, the males die, and then the daughters devour their mother and emerge pregnant.

Whatever the origin of death, whatever the parental expenditure, this is the bottom line: the relationship between mother and child is distinctly different than the relationship between child and mother. Mother names the child; for the child, mother has no other name.

Down an old woods road, beyond the neighbor's house, was a hill my father took us to for sledding. At the bottom were a ditch and a bank, deep enough and steep enough that you never popped up in front of a car on your sled, but were stopped or slid back down in the same kind of pendulous motion that was afforded on the vine in the woods.

One day, the neighbor boys had left the inflated tube of a tractor tire at the top of the hill. Lying across it and attempting to slide down the hill the way that was intended, in this particular snow, proved unproductive. But we knew how to travel; I had swung naked on a vine; we knew how this thing functioned. So, one at a time, we would curl up inside the middle and roll down the hill, like Scout in To Kill a Mockingbird, on her way, unaware, to Boo Radley's.

On one of these trips I spilled out of the middle before I'd intended, having hit a rock or a mogul, and as I did, my upper incisors came down hard on something; I split my lip with my own teeth. It swelled immediately, and we rushed back to the house, I pausing to spit blood into the snow at the place where the field funneled back into the old woods road. My mother called the doctor, who said—though the cut was probably deep enough to need it—they could not stitch the pink part of the lip. It would have to seal on its own. So I observed the kitchen sideways, sipping soup through the corner of my mouth, my head tilted parallel to the floor, trying to keep the salt from the wound. I harbored the gash like new terrain, two throbbing hills with a moist crevasse between. I can still feel the hard scar tissue deep in my lip; it had formed like a new and difficult word, the story of what could happen, what had happened, which I would deliver nonchalantly when I returned to school. Later that day, we would go back to the trail's end and look at the blood I had spit into the snow. It had frozen there like a track, a trail, an animal sign, a sign that we were on the move.

In the 1920's, five years after it was discovered that the red ant, Myrmica sabuletti, was a host to the large blue, scientists made an attempt to preserve the butterfly and its host by fencing in a nature reserve. Fencing in the reserve, however, excluded grazing animals. Without grazing animals, vegetation in the reserve grew unchecked. Unbeknownst at the time to the scientists, M. sabuletti would not build nests beneath plants over five centimeters high. With their host parents absent from the reserve, the large blue had no one to care properly for its young. Although individual members of other species of red ants were sometimes convinced by the large blue caterpillar's red ant larva act, the caterpillars adopted by these worker ants always died or were killed after being taken back to the nests.

We are all changelings. In Grimm's fairy tale, if a changeling laughs, it will be replaced by the original infant. A mother is told to boil water in egg shells over the fire; when she does, her changeling giggles and many tiny goblins arrive. They take it away and replace it with her original child. Perhaps this is why parents take such great pains to make their children smile: to ensure that whatever sacrifice is to come—at worst, being devoured from the inside—it is for the good of their own.

Perhaps we should have treated the large blue with the same patience we give to our own children when we allow them to step over cords, ford creeks, close doors. For a child's ridiculous rituals and games will eventually turn to determined choices—choices of lover and vocation. We are ourselves from the beginning. The large blue mother leaves her child in the womb, and then the home, of another. Like my sisters and I, like all children, the large blue is a traveler from birth. How could we have imagined that to confine her would save her? Instead, it belittled her, turned her polished act into a death sentence.

Our actions toward earth have been like child's play: a key thrown toward some unfamiliar door, only with no way to get it back, as if there were no strings attached. We have acted as if each thing that happens did not lead reasonably to another, heard the story all wrong: Fence! Fence! Come down; animals won't graze land; ants won't build nests; caterpillar can't fool parents. The roles must reverse. We must begin to treat earth not as mother, but as child, as we do our own children; for whom the rules we create and the boundaries we put up do not really prevent anything. We must promise to protect, but never to enclose, we must allow things to continually open and move, or we may find them going farther from us than we ever imagined they could.

[6] How Fluid My Body

I remember glimpsing the scattered, glossy pages from the bridge—where a friend would remain, too self-disciplined for an up-close look—and the half-hour I stood, knee-deep in water, reading, out-of-order, what men and women did, examining how they changed. I brought the pages, singly, into focus, then thrust them back below the surface again. In that creek, the water opened at the backs of my knees and closed again around the caps; when I emerged that day my legs left two holes in the current which I would use for years to study something larger than life, magnified by water and memory.

When I was a child, my family's home was full of solids. Some were obvious: bureaus, canned goods, closets packed with labeled boxes. Others were more hidden: the curious, curved metal legs and plastic wheels of the beds, on which we stubbed our toes, where we thought there was just space.

Liquids, on the other hand, were a safely guarded

commodity. My family cried over spilt milk, cups knocked over at the dinner table. No drinks were allowed in the living room. They were had only in the kitchen, and Popsicles only on the porch. Even when my sisters and I were too old to share a bath, we still shared the water—the last scrubbing in the cool, washed dirt of the second and first.

There were lapses, of course, all of them deliberate, and most having to do with what liquids my sisters and I could find either in the house when my parents were not around, or in the forest outside our home: in Dixie cups we created potions, filling them with water and baby powder, rubbing alcohol, mustard, and stirring with a Q-tip. Then, for fear we had produced not a cure for some malady, as intended, but a dangerous poison—or hearing our parents' car in the driveway—we poured them quickly down the drain. And there was a tryst of trees in the woods, whose shared trunk filled after rain and stayed full for weeks. We called the mystery it held "witches' brew." We added leaves, and stirred with a broken stick. Once, for some game, we filled a plastic container with cow's corn and mixed it with water. I entered the shed a few weeks later and smelled something that my parents, Methodists, did not drink, and so I could not identify. It smelled powerful and new. Horrified, I inspected the numerous primitive stems and roots on the kernels, that I, that the water, that secret ingredient, had produced.

But most of our encounters with water had to do with the stream, the same where I would later find the ripped-up girlie magazine. We grew up between the east and west branches of the Patapsco River, and had only to walk a half mile east or west from our back or front door to have lunch, or an adventure, near one of them. Occasionally, we picnicked upon a large cube-shaped rock far downstream on the west branch. Once, sitting atop it, I dropped a peeled orange into the water by accident. My sister instinctively flew downstream to retrieve it, and minutes later, I was biting into the fruit she handed me, heavy with creek. She did this not out of kindness or duty, but simply, I believe, because we wanted to keep what was ours. For even at that age, we knew what water did: water changed things. It brought them, and carried them away, sometimes irretrievably.

In the life cycle of some animals, the change from juvenile to adult is rather quick. Such metamorphoses, or concentrated periods of postembryonic development, are most often associated with butterflies. But metamorphosis occurs in nearly all insects, as well as in fish, amphibians, mollusks (such as snails), crustaceans, cnidarians (such as jellyfish), echinoderms (such as starfish), and tunicates (such as sea squirts).

Metamorphosis does not occur in birds, reptiles, or mammals, which includes humans, despite the fact that the bodies of these animals do change as they grow and become sexually mature. A just-hatched chickadee is structurally the same as its parents, although it cannot yet fly; a just-hatched garter snake looks even more like its parents, although it will likely not reach sexual maturity for three or four years, and a newborn infant, who may not reach sexual maturity until age ten for girls, and three to five years later for boys, is also structurally identical to its parents.

But a caterpillar, as everyone knows, looks vastly different from what it will look like as an adult. It has a long, segmented body with several pairs of legs and prolegs, rather than just the three it will have after metamorphosis; biting mouthparts rather than the sucking mouthparts of the adult; and a spinneret, which the adult butterfly lacks altogether, and which the caterpillar will use to spin the cocoon in which it will experience its sudden change. There, in the cocoon, the caterpillar produces enzymes that will digest most of its body. The unspecialized cells that remain will produce parts for eating and locomotion that the caterpillar probably never could have imagined operating.

The young of other animals which go through metamorphosis can look even more radical when compared to their adult forms. A young salamander looks like a tiny fish with a lion's mane of gills framing its narrow head. The larval stage of a sea squirt looks like a tadpole. It does not feed, but exists only for dispersal, and the stage ends once the larva finds a rock on which to cement itself. Then, because the adult is sedentary—a barrel-shaped, ocean floor filter-feeder—the larva digests the portion of its brain used to regulate movement. Starfish larvae look something like Sputnik, more crazily armed than they will ultimately end up. Snail larva, sporting multiple, symmetrical curling arms, or transparent, jelly-like, multi-petaled bodies, look like they don't want to retreat into the shells they have already begun to secrete, Only the fish and crustaceans look to me like they know where they are going, what they are going to become: small, see-through swimmers to larger, scaled ones; tiny, antennaed, multi-segmented-legged drifters, to hard-shelled, colored scuttlers. Still, even some of them experience quite unimaginable transformations. The flatfish has eyes on both sides of its head as a larva, but when it metamorphoses, one eye migrates until both eyes, perch-like, are on its left side. Imagine being able to see things from both sides as a child and then, suddenly, only from one. Would it be just you that had changed? Or would it be the whole world?

Dr. John Nash McDowell, of St. Louis, Missouri, founder of the Missouri Medical College in the early 19th century, was eccentrically concerned with a certain kind of change: the decay of the human body after death. More specifically, he was bothered by the inevitable postmortem decay of the bodies of his family members—something with which he may have been well-acquainted due to his complicity in obtaining specimens, for the illegal practice of dissection, by grave-robbing with his students. It is not apparent whether Dr. McDowell received any comfort from spirituality, from the believed eternal life of the souls of his kin, only that he had clear intentions to preserve their deceased bodies. McDowell planned to encase each departed family member in a copper tube in a solution of alcohol, and install him or her in a specially-designed niche in the medical school's tower.

When his 14-year-old daughter died from pneumonia, McDowell did place her in a chemical solution in a copper tube. But instead of depositing her into the heart of the medical school, he suspended the tube from the roof of a cave in the nearby town of Hannibal, on the banks of the Mississippi River. It was a cave he had purchased as a place for experimentation, where he believed the cool, stable temperature would aid in the preservation of the bodies he worked on. The daughter hung there for nearly a year, until locals heard about her from their children—including young

Sam Clemens, who wrote about his encounters with the encapsulated girl in Life on the Mississippi.

Imagine the children sneaking into the cave, swapping ghost stories, and spooking one another by slipping away from the back of the group down a passage and then appearing again suddenly in the front, coming upon this spectacle: a girl their own age, whom they did not recognize, seeming to hover between the rock walls. It must have taken a moment to realize that the girl, closed-eyed, so well-preserved that she was nearly blushing, could be seen only by their own candlelight, that she had no light of her own, and that she rested, at the peak of her adolescence, under water and under glass. Knowledge of her magnified once they left the cave, and the townspeople insisted on his taking her away, for they and the children found her petrifying. And the young McDowell was nearly petrified; upon removal, it is said, her body showed no signs of decay.

Next to the butterfly, the frog is probably the second best-known example of metamorphosis in the animal world. But a whole host of physical changes occur in the frog during metamorphosis beyond the easily observed growth of hind and front legs, and the gradual re-absorption of the tail. The frog's skin thickens, developing glands that will keep the skin from drying out while on land. Gills and gill slits are lost and lungs form, enabling the frog to mine oxygen from the air. The lateral line—a method of sensing motion in water—is lost, the shape of the nose changes and the middle ear forms, allowing for the frog to hear. Eyelids develop, the shape of the lens changes in the eye, and the eyes migrate to enable binocular vision, which the frog will need to catch prey. Skull bones form, the jaw lengthens, and the sticky tongue takes shape, ready to unroll and snag passing insects. The intestines shrink in order to better digest them.

The end result is something quite different from the juvenile, the tadpole, almost a different animal. Tadpoles are swimming, waterbound, suspension-feeding herbivores. Adult frogs are hopping, land-dwelling, predatory carnivores. Metamorphosis is more than just a change in physical features. It almost always occurs with changes in habitat and behavior.

In my house, it seemed, change came only by decree: you couldn't even go through puberty until my mother said so. That meant waiting for her permission to do all of the things I considered steps in reaching the status of my older sisters: closing the doors of certain rooms, wearing deodorant, shaving my legs. Just about the only thing my mother couldn't command with a few words was the onset of menses. Yet there was a time when I sat with my back to the full length mirror tacked to my bedroom door, opened my legs to a small lamp whose shade I had temporarily removed, and commanded the mass of skin that this procedure revealed to produce.

It was not entirely my mother's fault that I needed her blessing in order to mature sexually. In fifth grade, I needed my mother to notice the two new tumors on my chest to make certain they were breasts, so I thrust them at her while she brushed her teeth one evening and I was leaving the bath. (This was, apparently, before the closed door stage and, perhaps, was what justified it.) Likewise, when at the predicted age of twelve-and-a-half I awoke to find a sprinkle of brown blood in my underwear, I did not scamper off to the bathroom to take care of it, but waited through a full day of school. Then, in the evening, carrying the evidence, I crept to the kitchen, where my mother stood cooking dinner at the stove. Unable to find words for what was happening or the voice to convey them, I thrust the rusty cotton panel, spread like webbing between my fingers, towards my mother, and I waited, fixed, for her directions.

In May of 1747, explorer Captain Francis Smith, on his boat, the California, exploring near the Arctic Circle, wrote about the emergence of "an infinite Number of Frogs, with a great croaking." The frogs had survived the winter in holes in the ground, entirely frozen. "A remarkable Experiment," wrote Smith, "is to take the Earth in which the Frog is so froze, and to break that Earth in Pieces without thawing it, the Frog will then break with it as short as a Piece of Glass. But...lay that Earth at a small Distance from the Fire, so as to thaw it, the Frog will recover his Summer Activity, and leap as usual."

As if it weren't enough to change once, from the fish-like, one-gilled, head-bodied tadpole to the four-legged, lunged, tail-less frog, some species of frogs must change repeatedly each winter also, such as the wood frog, the one Captain Smith encountered, whose range crosses into the sometimes bitter cold Arctic Circle. In winter, the wood frog nearly changes from one state of matter to another, from, as Captain Smith described, liquid to solid.

Wood frogs hibernate in the soil under logs or leaves. In their winter places, well within the frost line, the frogs must give in to the temperatures around them. Because of their permeable skin, the frost that forms in the soil and leaves of their nestling grounds also immediately starts to form within them. When the temperature dips too low for too long, ice forms under their skin and around their stomachs. Ice crystals develop in the spaces around organs, and in the spaces between cells. Up to 70% of the water in the wood frogs' bodies becomes solid.

This would happen eventually to any immobile, cold-blooded animal in below-freezing surroundings, and would normally be followed by death from dehydration. But the liver of a wood frog has evolved to respond to the natural progression of freezing the frog can expect multiple times per year where it nestles within the frost line. When freezing starts to occur, the wood frog's liver produces extra sugars and packs them inside the cells. There, the sugars bind onto water, which lowers its freezing point and keeps the water from flooding through the cell membranes and causing dehydration, and then forming tiny ice crystals which would rupture the frog's tissues in a massive, deadly case of frostbite.

It may take up to twenty-four hours for total freezing to occur in a wood frog, when the heart stops and the brain begins to rely on anaerobic respiration because without blood circulating, of course, it lacks oxygen. But when temperatures rise, it takes only a few hours to return to the living—the frog's heartbeat and circulation resume before all of the ice in the body has melted; the back legs move after just a couple of hours. And in less than a week, the frog can be ready for mating.

I'm impressed with how these creatures can change all their lives, from tadpole to frog, from liquid to solid, and back to liquid again. I search for them on the frozen forest floor, like one article I read suggests, hoping to find what Captain Smith found, these little nuggets of life, safe and still, evidence that change is easy, that it's possible to endure many thaws and freezes.

With metamorphosis there often comes a change in habitat, and I will make a series of moves on my way to love, engagement, and marriage. At one stop, I'll be five hours north of where I grew up, lower in the watershed, next to the Hudson River, a river fifty times as wide and as deep as either the east or the west branch of the Patapsco, a river that is sometimes brackish, and subject to tides, and, therefore—although I will wait for it to, will walk there every evening in winter—doesn't freeze completely.

The children whom I will teach at my job will assure me that at one time the river here did freeze all winter long and all the way across. They will pummel me with facts I feel I should know, but are strange to me, because they are not my local history: to protect themselves from the British during the revolution, they will tell me, the colonists dragged huge iron spikes out upon this river's ice. In spring, when the ice melted and the river was flowing, the spikes were still there, solidly sunk to the bottom, protecting the inhabitants of the coastal towns by threatening to pierce the hulls of any ships that dared to venture near them. And, the children will relate, there were chains put across the river, with links three feet long and six inches thick. Then they'll throw out the nouns, cementing the moral of the story: the chains and the mountains and the spikes kept the towns safe, they'll say.

But I will walk to the river and watch it pouring through

patch-ice, shattering clear, brittle surfaces just two feet from its banks. For I must go home for solid things, imagining, as I drive through the night, the somewhat familiar names of the roads that will take me there in my father's voice, to prevent myself from becoming lost: Western Run, Tufton Avenue. Then, somehow, their exits become clear, fog lines defined, intersections meet, instead of seeming to lead nowhere. Once home, I creep through my parents' house, secretly lifting, raising and lowering like weights the solids that I know will be there: potatoes on a shelf in the basement; in my father's drawer, two shiny pink cuff links on tiny green pillows; in addition, a cracked leather case containing the family's only set of nail clippers. In the hall closet, three irons. A piano and organ in the living room.

When I was a child, I could not travel far enough, could not figure out where the west branch of the Patapsco River came from or went to no matter how fast I walked before dinner. Nor could I imagine how fluid my body must have seemed to my mother and father, like a spilled drink escaping carelessly and swiftly from its container from the instant I was born, for to me it seemed straight and thin and flat, and could not change fast enough. Now, I feel like I can't stop myself from going, from moving away from my childhood home. I long for those icons of history to keep me in, like the spikes that kept the residents of the Hudson Valley safe during the Revolution, and those matriarchal decrees—the rules my mother made that drew clear boundaries between the forms that matter could take and the places it could be—the ability, like the wood frog, to transform back into something I once was, even if only temporarily. I long for something to cradle, something to hold or to hold me: heavy curtains to hang on a picture window, to close carefully, as my mother did, each night on my own family so that not even a sliver of light would leak from where we were to the outside. But mostly, I long for those two holes I put in the creek long ago to close, to heal, to bring into focus once and for all what the river had, and has, to show me.

[7] This Game

I learned to slice from a lover. He said, as I struggled with a mushroom, move the vegetable, not the knife, or you'll cut your thumb. He showed me how to keep the pointed end down against the cutting board, and slide the cap under. Neat slices fell to the right. I felt like a clock ticking off seconds: clean, efficient. I watched the knife pivot. Things moved more quickly. Then he left me for another.

I have learned to see the forest which surrounds my childhood home as a fragment—not a figment; it is there still—but as a fragment, a narrow crescent between our lawn and the cornfields to the north and northeast, whereas once it was huge and held us, held us all, endlessly.

I have learned to see it as a slice left from what our forefathers found when they arrived: virtually unbroken forest from the shores of the Atlantic to the Mississippi. I have learned, thanks to a course in conservation biology, that leaving this slice—and others—most certainly increased the amount of edge along what was once unbroken interior:

trees and trees and trees for miles and miles.

Do the math. Draw a square that is 6" by 6" and calculate the perimeter. Calculate the area. You should come up with 24 inches of perimeter and 36 square inches of area. Now imagine that three new roads have been cut across this little plot of land. Divide your square into three long rectangles, or fragments, each about 2" by 6". This habitat loss, in itself, is why we no longer see an interior creature such as the wolf in the place where I grew up: Finksburg, Maryland. But the problem goes much deeper.

Although not much physical space may be lost by a road-cut—the area of each new rectangle is still about 12 square inches—there is quite a bit more perimeter in three small plots of land than in one large one. In the 6" by 6" plot of land the ratio of perimeter to area is 24 to 36 or, reduced, 4 to 6. In the second example, after the road-cuts, the ratio of perimeter to area in each fragment is 16 to 12 or, reduced, 4 to 3. It has nearly doubled; instead of 4 inches of perimeter for every 6 square inches of land, there is now 4 inches of perimeter for every 3 square inches of land.

Forest fragmentation not only reduces populations of creatures that require large, unbroken tracts of land for home ranges, but also increases habitat for edge-loving animals: rabbits, squirrels, fox, deer—all the game animals of our grandfathers. Forest fragmentation doesn't just result in less nature; it makes nature different.

So what if we sacrifice a wolf for a couple of deer? Has it hurt anything other than the rosebush in your front lawn, browsed bud-less by the innocent whitetail before it can bloom? Once my lover told me he liked the edges of things, as he traced the seam of my sleeve. And it is precisely at this time, when one falls in love, where before one has simply grown up in it, that edges—beginnings and endings—begin.

I should have learned to slice from my mother, long before I was making pizzas with a man twice my age. For it was she who taught me first about wholes, and pieces. My youth is marked by the things she cut: grapes, celery, bangs.

Recently I was making a recipe for chicken salad that included split grapes. I reached for one of the grapes as I cut them. The flat side against my mouth brought me back to the time when my mother knew the way I laughed and ran as I ate, the shape of my esophagus, my impatience. She sliced the grapes for my sisters and me without complaint. She also gave us cold bowls of celery sliced carefully into half-centimeters, lightly salted. She did this, she says, because she needed to get fiber in us. The pieces of celery looked like short, fat inchworms. She called them "cuttin' worms" and we believed her.

When my sister got braces, she couldn't eat our summer staple. I watched for weeks this duet at the dinner table: my sister would butter and salt her corn on the cob as my mother stood next to her, grim, waiting. Then mother slid the knife down the cob in great premeditated strokes; the corn came off in great rows. I bore the whole presentation in agony, thinking, how can it taste the same in a pile on her plate? On her spoon?

My mother also cut in other rooms. She cut my bangs in a half moon. I remember the cold quarter-inch of the sewing scissors on my forehead, close enough to be invisible.

But eventually we had to beg, when we were grown, when we were able to reason that an apple tasted better in eighths. This is when she began to say no.

And so did I, for to keep things pure you must eventually say no. To keep things whole you must leave them whole, digest them whole, use patience and strength, and accept a bit of bitter peel with every bite. You must not take things in doses, expect them to add up to more than they are, to cure. Think of the first time your mother cut for you, when you were cut from her: it was letting you go, but it brought you into her world.

Our forest has not become smaller. No trees have been taken in the last twenty-five years, except by gypsy moths, and these have been replaced by blackberry bushes, for a while. It's just that when we were younger, we didn't see the sizes of things. We didn't go through the forest; we went in. And if we went from one end of the forest to the other, still we were not going through; we were simply going into something larger, a place that encompassed our forest, the two cornfields behind it, the wooded corridor that separated them, and the creek in the valley beneath.

Edges make the brown-headed cowbird happy. The cowbird has evolved a unique way of ensuring that it passes on its genes. It flies around the edges of things—fields, and forests, looking for the nests of smaller birds: flycatchers, finches, vireos, warblers. Then it deposits one of its own eggs in each nest it finds. This is, for the most part, unbeknownst to the host, the owner of the nest, who, when the eggs hatch, will raise the cowbird as, and often instead of, her own. The reason the cowbird doesn't pick on somebody her own size: most birds, programmed to respond to the squawking of their hungry young according to volume, feed the loudest—the baby cowbird—most and more often. Other brood parasites—the European cuckoo and the African honeyguide, have evolved even more horrific ways of ensuring that they alone are raised by their foster parents. The cuckoo, just after hatching, before it can open its eyes, jerks and heaves its body in a series of specific, intricate moves which result in knocking other eggs and young out of the nest. The honeyguide uses its hooked bill to murder any nest mates.

Many birds do not recognize that the cowbird egg is not their own. Others who do simply cannot remove it from the nest. The yellow warbler, however, upon finding a cowbird egg in her nest, will build a new floor of twigs and gray grass and mud, covering the unwanted cowbird egg and, unfortunately, also some of her own. Warbler nests have been found with six layers of new floors, each with its own cowbird egg support.

Because they frequent forest edges, brown-headed cowbird populations have skyrocketed in recent decades. A fair number of the birds upon which cowbirds prey used to remain safe by nesting in the forest interior, but without large tracts of forest left, more and more songbirds find themselves raising not their own young but the hatchling from a cowbird egg instead, causing declines in their own populations. Increased edges don't obliterate nature, necessarily, but jumble things, causing some species to thrive, and pushing others to their limit.

In the beginning I met my lover at the creek, on the railroad tracks that split the forest between our houses in half, where bulldozers and backhoes had been brought in to replace the ties and repair the rails after a flood twenty years ago had made them impassable. A few years later, when we wanted to attend a Christmas Eve service together, he drove me to a church over the state line. For summer vacation we drove three hours to the shore, crossed over to an island, and I read him poetry on the beach.

We were surprised when two people we both knew emerged from the sea, a father—his friend—and a daughter—my schoolmate. They were almost unrecognizable, wet, dark hair on pale heads, pale skin streaming out of swimsuits. The girl's locks were curled into question marks around her eyes as she tried to make certain who I was; but he and I together must have been harder to identify, a nonnative species skirting the edge as if it were where we belonged, as if it were somewhere we could hide.

When we decided, after many years, that it wasn't, that staying always on the edge didn't provide enough cover, I couldn't think of anything to say. A few days later, in a kind of trance, I ran deep into the forest and pulled up a plant of wild ginger, a shade-lover, with its brown, jug-shaped flower hidden beneath ever-green, heart-shaped leaves. I drove to his house, and carried the plant up to his room to leave beside his bed in a little pot, offering one small bit of the interior to pass between us.

I've always been wary of edges, if I was aware of them at all. When my sisters and I stood, brushing our teeth at the two sinks in our bathroom, I in the center, my sisters would scold me for squeezing the toothpaste tube from the middle. They insisted that a set of directions on the toothpaste tube itself actually advised to squeeze the tube from its end. I didn't believe them, so they unrolled the tube and pointed to the sentence. But their fingernails underlined something that was yet foreign to me: my own language, a series of hard marks and swirls, like a shattered grid of tic-tac-toe, a web I had swung my hand into to clear a path in the woods. I squinted at the letters, unable to believe that one day I would be able to read, or that my sisters were telling the truth.

Soon enough, though, while my sisters were at school, my mother would fill a nine inch square cake pan with three or four rows of wooden blocks, then turn a few of the blocks so their letters, together, made a familiar series of sounds—somewhere in the interior of the wood, amid a scramble of color, a word would form: there would appear a "cat" or a "dog."

Learning to read, falling in love, these are the ways edges begin. For when you are young a story is full and never leaves—just a breath can bring it about. But a chapter already divides; it becomes tiresome, dog-eared, a stretched spine. Love can become a cliff we want to jump off of all too fast. This is how we punctuate our lives.

Once, I sat with my two-year-old nephew in the grass. He ordered me, "Play." I said, "What are we playing?" He said, "A game." Always needing all the facts, I asked, "What game?" He replied, "This game." And that is a child—the world has no beginning, no setting up; we are simply in it, playing already.

Nearly ten years later, one of my sisters wants to take her children down to the creek where we used to play. No more forest has been lost, but the fields have become yards, and we feel too old to trespass. We set out, both sisters and I, and three of their children, venturing into a slice of woods only peripherally explored, in search of an old path. The woods are thick with sticker-bushes and, carrying the little ones, we persevere with fervor, trying to transport our children back in time. After a half hour both my sisters and my two youngest nieces—two and five—turn back. But the eleven-year-old and I press on, finding the path, and the creek, and an easier way home; one of the fields has not yet been turned into a yard, and there's corn planted on a steep slope up from the creek to our house, and my nephew says with confidence: along the edge of every cornfield, there's a path. He's right.

We return to the house and eat lunch, then bring the five-year-old back down. But on the way home my niece and nephew want to walk in the corn, going rows deeper until we've crested the hill entirely within the crop. My nephew says, "Did you learn anything today?" I search my brain, not knowing what he means, what he's referring to, and he offers, "On the edge of every cornfield there's a path."

But we didn't use the path going back. And what I can't forget is how, earlier, just after the others had turned back, after my nephew and I had climbed up from a dry streambed we thought would lead us to the creek, we found ourselves in a low grove of shrubs, whose leaves had yellowed from the shade of taller trees above. I could hardly stand up. The sun was shining through, and my nephew stopped and commented on the color of the light in this dense part of the woods. We were deep inside, it was special, and he knew it.

I am asking you to stay in it. Surround yourself with something, and not just to seek its parameters. Be a creature of the interior. Don't stretch it, but use it to its fullest extent. Don't look through it; look deeper and deeper. Continue. Make sure you are looking for more, and not for an end or a beginning.

[8] Sugaring Off

The pith of the staghorn sumac is so soft, colonial farmers could easily hollow out short lengths of sumac branches with a hot iron poker. This created perfect little spouts through which the sap could run from maple trees into the farmer's buckets. The soft-hearted sumac, sometimes considered a shrub and sometimes a small tree, rarely grows beyond the size of a sapling; farmers took advantage of this fact when choosing wood for spiles. For when a tree reaches a certain size, some parts of it slowly begin to die, hardening both inside and out, making it difficult to hollow. The heartwood toughens, deep in the core, where living xylem once carried water from the roots to the leaves. The bark of the tree also becomes lifeless, harboring dead phloem cells, which once carried food from the leaves throughout the tree. Only a narrow band of living tissue persists, in a mature tree, between the bark and the heartwood. It produces each year a brand new layer of xylem on the inside and one of phloem on the outside. Nonetheless, a mature tree could not survive without its dead apportionments. They've done their share of lifting and rendering, stretching and bending. Far from useless, now they simply refuse to give in, standing tall and firm, protecting the tree from all kinds of invasions.

One day I was lying, as all girls do at some watershed in their lives, barefoot, in cut-offs and a white t-shirt, on the cool ledge of a bridge at the intersection of two roads, a creek, and a set of railroad tracks. Cars sped by me on one side, and water on the other. At this early time, it was not the car that was familiar but the driver. He waved and pointed to the general store, which sat on the side of the bridge from which I had come.

Without thinking, I leapt down onto the road to head for the store. The pavement was unforgivingly hot, but instead of putting on my shoes—spray-painted black, Converse All-star high-tops, cut off to make them ankle height—and proceeding calmly forward, I deliberately carried them in my hand, hopping and skipping through his rearview mirror. All the way to the store, like a prop, like bait, the shoes danced in my fingers. As I waited in the cool grass for him to emerge, the bottoms of my feet smarting and misunderstood, I realized that it had been a mistake; I saw that I should have put my shoes on. But I still stood there, dangling them in my right hand as he walked down the old stone steps, my naked legs leading directly into the soil.

In Spanish class, I found a word for where I liked to sit in my girlhood. In my tenth-grade textbook, an illustration at the start of each chapter introduced the vocabulary for the week. One day, the picture showed a woman leaning over the ledge of a bridge. The ledge was waist-high, made of stone, and underneath, water streamed. Antepecho, the text said, next to the stone ledge. Looking at the picture was like looking into a mirror.

The average Spanish-English dictionary defines antepecho as simply a sill or a railing, but the place I liked to walk to, and the place in the picture, was neither. A sill implies something upon which you might leave a pie to cool, or set a potted plant, rest only your forearms; a railing brings to mind something skeletal, around which you might wrap just a hand. The ledge of the bridge I walked to was wide and solid, and I would sit on it sometimes with both feet hanging dangerously over the water, my back to the passing cars.

Each illustration usually involved two people—Maria and Juan, or Maria and Felipe. In this one, I seem to remember Juan beneath the bridge, retrieving something for Maria—a flower or bag that she had accidentally dropped over the antepecho. Flor, the book would have said, or bolso, each item so easily identified, words that my adolescent mind grouped into perhaps more meaningful combinations than they were intended to be. Uninterpreted, though, were the characters' expressions, their intentions. Was Maria in distress or gratitude? Was Juan courting Maria? And if he was, why was he hunched over, exiting the arched opening beneath the bridge like a troll?

In Canada some years, the maples burst in spring. This would probably be April or May up there, when the temperatures at night still drop well below freezing, but during the day they soar to forty and above. The fluctuating temperatures cause the vessels within the tree to contract during the cold nights and then expand in the sun's heat, creating a suction that fills the xylem with stored sap from the roots. Sometimes the expansion is so great that the tree actually bursts. The bark gives way with a pop as startling as a gunshot and sap begins to drip surely from its seams.

There weren't many maples where I grew up, and anyway the temperatures were too relatively moderate there to rupture them. Sugar maples and red maples range south from Canada all the way to Florida and west to North Dakota and Eastern Texas. But sugar maples prefer uplands and are mostly found in the higher elevations of the Southern states. I can only remember two specific maples. One was next to our driveway, and one was outside my sisters' bedroom window.

I remember them both because they were very young, and unlike the looming chestnut oaks and numerous Black locusts in our yard, their bark was smooth and seamless. I remember that the trunk of the one by our driveway had divided in two, and I remember the one outside my sisters' bedroom window because we used to climb it, although I don't know how; the branches are too high up for me to reach even now. There must have been lower branches that died and broke off, shaded out by the newer, higher ones, for the branches that I see on that maple now could never have been reachable from the ground. Trees do not grow like humans, their branches getting progressively higher from the earth, like a toddler's arms. Trees grow from the tops of their heads and the tips of their fingers and their toes, which would make an odd-looking human, who grows—physically at least—proportionately, everything in order.

I waited for him to come out of the general store on a

grass plot above the creek where someone had planted an orchard tree. On the ground surrounding my naked feet was its rotting fruit: tiny peaches, so small that no one would eat them.

That day, he came over and stood by me on the grass, trying to hide something behind his back—two cartons of cigarettes—and at the same time complimenting me on some poem of mine that had come across his desk. He offered me a ride home, and although I wasn't headed there, wasn't planning on leaving the ledge of the bridge where I had been sitting for hours, still holding the shoes, I accepted and left with him.

At my house, he came inside and sat down and met my mother. She was reading the newspaper. In our living room, in front of both of us, he continued to afford me the highest praise. My mother nodded, pleased and polite. But even at that early point, and even to me, his entrance into our house seemed odd, bold. The confidence with which he spoke of me, one of the members of the household, within its own four walls, seemed uncharacteristic of a visitor. We did not know it at the time, but on that hot summer day, we had both been taken; he had somehow gained permission to enter my life.

During every season, some part of the red maple is red. In summer it is the petioles, the slender filaments which attach each leaf to the branch. In fall, of course, it is the leaves themselves. In winter it is next year's buds. And in spring it is the tiny flowers that you will not notice until they fall, wilted, all over your driveway and car.

When I was in high school, there was a mass movement among the English teachers to grade in green. Grading in red was like bleeding on the page, they said all of a sudden. Even A's seemed to come from somewhere too passionate, too violent. Steeped in symbolism, red ink was courageously abandoned and papers instead came flying back at me in the color of envy, the color of spring.

According to the Anishinabe of the Great Lakes region, maple trees used to be filled, year-round, with thick syrup. This was when the world was new, when there was an abundance of game and good weather, and life was very easy. One day, Manabozho, a trickster god, came looking for his people. He couldn't find them anywhere—they were not planting in the fields, fishing in the lakes or streams, or gathering berries in the forest. When he finally came upon them, he was disgusted. They were in the maple grove, lying on their backs with their mouths wide open under broken branches they had snapped off themselves in order to catch the sweet syrup that ran from them. Manabozho, who could not stand to see his people become so fat and lazy, filled a birch basket many times with water, climbed up to the tops of the maples, and poured the water down inside the branches, diluting the syrup. He also caused the sap to run only at one time of year, in the spring, before the buds opened. And so it is, to this day.

If you break the twig of a sugar maple on a cool spring day and taste a drop of the sap that drips from it, it will taste only very faintly sweet. Sugar maple sap contains just 2-4% sugar. The sap of a red maple may contain a half percent less, and the sap of a silver maple a half percent less than that.

This means they would both require more boiling to thicken them up into something you would want to pour over your pancakes, or use to baste a ham. Most commercial operations tap only sugar maples, but where sugar maples can't be found, some will tap a red. Hardly anyone taps silver, unless there is no other option. I have made syrup from all three, and found each satisfactory.

I try to imagine what I must have looked like that afternoon in front of the general store: tan, in white and blue, with no hem on my shorts and no seams on my shoes and my shoes in my hand, running toward him. He was wearing flip-flops. We stared down at the grass to avoid acknowledging the hidden cigarettes, and instead caught our naked feet staring back up at us. Somehow, this was worse.

Soon, he would listen to me read in a city café to which he had driven me, and engrave the date into the spoon he used there to add cream and sugar to his coffee. It was something he could package up in a gold colored box on a length of cotton, suited for a necklace, and pass me in the hall to unwrap in Latin class, and be stirred, inescapably.

There were things he and I both loved—music and words—and there were things he wanted to do after that day which, at that age, I simply couldn't understand: grow herbs in a little garden, plant ornamental trees, identify birds in the yard. Eastern hemlocks he had mentioned more than once, lamenting the fact that they didn't grow below the Mason-Dixon line—except in the mountains—like they did in, say, Connecticut, somewhere he might like to live. At that time, I just didn't know the names of things. I had no text to label, in italics, what was happening.

Now, on two different days in the forest, on nearly the same branch, just a few feet in front of and above me, there lands, first, a rose-breasted grosbeak, and later, a ruby-throated hummingbird. Some things I still don't know what to call, but I know these two now easily: one wears its red like a jewel, the other like it's nearly been murdered. I also know the maple, with its egg-shaped silhouette, even branching, bright autumn leaves.

I'm just a few degrees north in latitude now and there are maples all around me. So, religiously, the first week of March, which is early spring right about here, like those colonial farmers, I drill little holes in them and put buckets beneath. Unfailingly, they give me what is hidden. The fruit of this tree is not obvious, not sweet. I can stand and watch the sap drip from the spile in a maple tree for twenty minutes. But longer is the time I spend boiling away the excess, all that simple water to get the pint or quart of syrup that promises to unveil itself from somewhere in the clear.

And I know the rules: a puncture no bigger than 7/16 of an inch, no deeper than two inches, leave the heartwood alone. And at the end of the season, do not seal the holes—we do not call them wounds. Let them heal in the open.

[9] Swingset Road

They've taken Fatso. We knew it would happen sooner or later. It occurred over a period of years, really. First the old barn fell, and left the crumpled metal roof too low to moan on windy nights. Next they filled in the well. Then they spent a summer thinning the forest. Whether this was for lumber or construction or both, we didn't know. But after a few months the backhoes were suddenly gone, everything toppled was left behind, and my sister and I fashioned a game that involved walking a circuitous route around and within that entire acre on fallen trees. We balanced on some and leapt to others; the object was never to touch the ground.

At that point, however, we still had Fatso, a large tree, whose broad, squarely curved branches, like high-backed chairs, held us upright while we sat in them to read. According to my father, there was a farmhouse in that corner of the woods once, and it faced the road we lived on when that road was just dirt. Another dirt road cut behind the farmhouse, separating it from Fatso, the well, and the barn.

This road is still evident on my parents' property.

Though my parents built their own house and grew our yard right upon it, the road still quite visibly disappears at our lawn and emerges again on the other side. At one time, one end of the road was bordered with a stone wall, quite an oddity for the state of Maryland, which was never glaciated, as well as for our region, which is about an hour from the rock-breeding Catoctin Mountains of the Appalachians. My parents always complained that our soil was too rocky for a garden, but it simply lacked the litter of large stones and the necessity of moving them that begets most walls, like the ones that begin to unravel in the northernmost counties of New Jersey and trek across the New England states. New Jersey is where I would first move for school after living for twenty-two years with my family on the footprint of this old farm. On the day I left, my mother stood in the driveway and prophesied, as if I were about to travel through time and not just space: "You're going to meet your future there and never come back."

The stone wall on my parents' property always appeared like a pile to me more than a wall, and it is difficult to remember what it looked like before the first time we dismantled it and used the stones to build something else— obstacles for a dirt bike trail, steps that led up to nothing and then back down again. We named both ends of the old dirt path—all 500 yards or so that were left—"Doghouse Road" and "Swingset Road" according to what we stationed upon them. For years they were the only place names we needed within our family to explain anything: where we were going, where we'd been, where something had happened.

Travel is always risky—for the living and, apparently,

also for the dead. There was some controversy around the recent decision of the Ethiopian government to transport the bones of Lucy, a very-nearly whole (by anthropological standards), 3.2 million-year-old skeleton of *Australopithecus afarensis*, an ancestor of modern humans, to the Houston Museum of Natural Science.

Since her discovery in 1974, Lucy has been housed in vaults in the National Museum in Addis Ababa, the capital of Ethiopia, the country in which her bones were discovered. Many scientists are in an uproar about her travel to the Houston Museum of Natural Science, citing a 1998 non-binding UNESCO resolution that suggests that hominid fossils remain in their home country and be transported only for scientific study and not for public viewing. They argue that Lucy's bones, which have fossilized to stone, are too fragile to withstand travel to the ten American museums scheduled to display her, that the six years of display unfairly remove her from scientific study, and that displaying her publicly is a form of prostitution of our human ancestors, enacted primarily to bring a windfall of money to participating museums and the Ethiopian government.

For her trip, Lucy traveled first class in two hard suitcases, each bone couched in museum quality foam in a specially carved slot.

The farmer who lived in the farmhouse on Swingset Road, my father has said, was found dead—of a heart attack, I suppose—on his tractor in the field. His house was torn down, but the barn was left alone, along with other clues that the land had been inhabited before we moved there. There were apple trees that we discovered deep in a nearby forest by the sweet, rotting remnants of their fruits on the ground. There were bluebells and daffodils that bloomed on their own in the woods that we awaited each spring, and a rosebush we forgot about until its flowers burst forth from a mass of poison ivy every Fourth of July. And quite often, I remember unearthing pieces of curved, white porcelain. At the time, I wanted to find a fossil. The smooth, faceless shards that I turned over in the soil with the toe of my tennis shoe, pausing from some game, only made me think of an angry wife shattering plates against a hearth; there was something too recent about broken dishware to make a collection of it.

But the most obvious clue that the land had belonged to someone before us was the old well. It lay right beneath Fatso. It was somehow more obvious than the barn. It seemed large for a well; it was probably six feet across. There was no protective, waist-high wall of stones surrounding it, nor was there evidence of a wooden structure having encircled it at some earlier point in time either. It simply opened from the forest floor, a wide dark circle in a mass of trailing vines and sticker-bushes. Oddly, we had no fear of falling in it. It seems we knew exactly where it was. Perhaps the distinct difference between the lush, thorny mat we cautiously picked our way through to get to Fatso and the smooth, black, empty space of the well was warning enough.

I barely remember being able to look down it. What I do remember is picnicking upon a wooden cover my father made for the well after a neighbor's puppy disappeared. In the end he made a raised wooden platform, carpeted it with tarpaper, and encircled the wide bottom with a skirt of wire mesh so that now even a very thin child could not slip through. As soon as it was finished—and to my mother's dismay, I'm sure—we immediately commenced to eat lunch and play cards and board games upon it. We basked in the sun there like snakes, waking only to push rocks through the wire mesh with just the right amount of force and then listening to hear the condition of the water: a small "Yup," sent patiently up to reassure us that it was, covered or not, still a well, a passage to something else. Beneath, it was full of risk, but above it was like a stage for us—the covered well—like a room in the forest, a smooth, flat, even surface where we could play like human children and yet never leave the woods.

Lucy's trip to the Houston Museum of Natural Science is not the first time she has traveled. Lucy was discovered in the Hadar region of Ethiopa by U.S. scientist Donald Johanson and his graduate student, Tom Gray. Taking a different route home from an area they had been mapping and surveying for fossils, Johanson noticed a human-like pelvis and rib lying out in the open. Further digging revealed several hundred bone fragments.

As discoverer, Johanson was allowed to take Lucy home to Cleveland to study her for several years. An August 28, 2007 article in the Chicago Tribune includes Johanson's description of Lucy's first trip: he wrapped her bones in toilet paper and foam padding, placed her in a hard case, and took her as carry-on luggage on several commercial flights.

Although technically she was being transported for scientific study, Lucy's first trip also resulted in her first public viewing. According to Johanson, a French customs official interested in archaeology—who had been informed of the recent discovery—actually had Johanson remove

Lucy's bones from their wrapping and lay them out on a table briefly for passengers to view. This was "much to their delight," reports the article.

But this story is about Fatso, who as I write this is completely gone. Fatso grew beside the well near Swingset Road, and had once had, at least in middle age, no competition on that farm in the denuded countryside. He may have been as good an example of an old-growth tree as one can get in central Maryland. I'm not sure when we discovered him, but I think he really belonged to my sister who, because of his girth, gave him his name.

Fatso could be climbed in only two ways. The first was the way my sister used: his lowest branch was actually a branch of a branch parallel to the ground—so high that it took a few leaps to wrap one's arms successfully around it. Wrapping the legs came next and then heaving the body up over the branch. At this point, the branches were so hefty that you could stand and walk your way to the first joint, and then the second. Fatso had spreading branches; we mounted him at least fifteen feet away from the trunk. The second way up I devised for myself, and probably to my sister's chagrin, when at four years younger I could not always jump to reach the branch she could just barely touch. Fatso had another branch that, though higher, was accessible by climbing a thicket of shrubs that grew beneath it, whose branches broke if you lingered on them too long. I would scuffle up this way while my sister, graceful and gymnastic, leapt and swung and curled herself to the top. When we had mastered this ascent, Fatso became another place on the map that allowed the members of my family our distance yet held us together. We were either "down Swingset Road" or "on Doghouse Road," or "over at Fatso."

Lucy has always been popular, even before her controversial second trip to America. Examination of her knee and hip joints upon discovery showed immediately that Lucy traveled on two feet. She could walk upright. In 1974, she was the oldest fossil the world had of a bipedal hominid.

Prior to Lucy's discovery, it was believed that humans began to walk upright after developing the especially large brains we currently have relative to body weight. The larger brains, scientists thought, resulted in the intellectual ability to use and design tools. This required the hands to be free. Apes able to spend more time on two feet because of normally negligible differences in anatomy—a slimmer pelvis, for instance—would proliferate because of the benefits of tool use. They would produce more children, who would out-compete their quadruped cousins.

But the cavity that held Lucy's brain was only the size of a softball. Thus, Lucy changed the order in the timeline of behaviors crucial in the evolution of modern humans: first came bipedalism, and only then larger brains. First travel, then intelligence. It has also been theorized that humans began walking on two feet due to climactic changes that thinned forests and increased the savannah, giving them, in effect, increased walking area and decreased swinging terrain. But at 3.2 million years old, Lucy shows that hominids were already walking on two feet long before these climactic changes occurred. In a way, she was "pre-adapted" to the more open environment in which her descendants would find themselves. We don't yet know why, but Lucy wanted to travel.

At one point, I thought I would never know what type of tree Fatso was. The old farm had been sold, my father called to tell me, the barn completely removed, and the forest cleared. I came home during that time to find a backhoe and port-o-potty parked on Swingset Road. I meant to go out and investigate, but it snowed, and I didn't have the right shoes or the right coat. So I thought I had given up my last chance to properly identify Fatso.

There were other trees we played on in our childhood, many of which are still there, still growing. And I can infer the identities of some without revisiting them. One had a first branch so high we had to climb a vine that hung along its straight trunk twenty feet up just to sit on it. In the spring this tree dropped orange and green flowers. Another I climbed high and carved into; its bark around the names of my first loves was smooth and gray. And then there was one that had been struck by lightning and felled at the very base. Part of its bark was blackened and peeling off in a thick chunk, but the rest was lined and papery and glinted silver under our toes as we walked up and down it, or sat upon it, clutching a small burl with both hands like a saddle horn. Even between shrubs we saw rooms and raked them out and played house; we picked and stacked in our hands their waxy, evergreen leaves and used them for tickets to circuses we put on for each other. Back then, trees were lookout towers, horses, houses, currency. But now I know them as tulip poplar, beech, birch.

But from Fatso, on the night my father called to tell me he was gone, I couldn't remember a leaf, or a flower, or even a seed. We knew him from the inside, from scrapes on our palms and wrists and arms, from brown stains on our jeans. The pattern in his bark—if there was one—seemed to reach farther than Doghouse or Swingset Road—too broad for us to interpret or map at that time. His silhouette was hidden by second-growth; we could only see his crown from within it; we knew him by his body, his bones. To try and describe him would have been like trying to describe the movement of the planets and stars from the earth. How many years did this take us? Somehow I couldn't put myself somewhere else to see him, outside of him to understand him. He still seemed like the center of something, although, cut down, he couldn't possibly be anymore.

When I was living on the footprint of the old farm, I wanted to find a fossil. I tried to make them at the creek, pressing a leaf in the mud for some future child to find atop a mountain or in a road cut, a child who would try hard to imagine something no longer in existence—our creek—once laying sediment there. At the time I was hoping somehow that the process might be sped up and I would find my own fossil, the imprint of an acorn on the stream bottom, but the creek was changed each time I visited, even though it looked the same to me; my projects in the mud disappeared whenever I left them.

I also believed I could make a diamond by placing a stolen charcoal from the family grill beneath the heaviest rock I could lift. I checked it every few days or so, trying not to lessen the pressure or interrupt the rearrangement of its atoms too often. I remember thinking that even if I did not experience the transformation, someone would, some lucky hiker in the next century or so who, walking with his head down, would suddenly be blinded by the reflection of the sun in the earth: the sparkle of a crude diamond. Like any child, I understood and affirmed life's processes. But I couldn't fathom the real mystery—the dimension of time. I still couldn't that day my mother stood in the driveway and said good-bye to me as I left our home for New Jersey, although by then I didn't lack knowledge of how long certain changes could take, but rather of the opposite: how fast life could be.

I did find a fossil, finally, after I moved permanently out of my parents' home to Pennsylvania with my new husband, whom, as my mother foretold, I met in New Jersey. Where I lived at this time, there was a small pull-off at the base of a hill on one side of the street I took home from work every day, and every so often I would see one or two cars parked there, at what appeared to be the start of an old woods road. One Saturday, prepared for a day hike, I parked at the spot and walked up the wide path to where it opened to a large outcrop of dark, extremely broken rock. At first, I walked through it and around it, searching for the other end of the woods road, for cairns that would tell me where to go, but the road seemed to stop at the unusual, bald mountain-top. All around, spring peepers chirped from hidden vernal pools—taunting me, path or no path, to explore the woods. But finally, I began to circle within it—this mass of black, cracked rock—walking with my head down, and there on the ground next to a small sapling was a curious-looking, tear-drop shaped rock with evenly segmented ridges on both sides: a fossil.

I sat down and put my hands, in gratitude, on the sun-warmed rocks. The fossil came home with me, and sat for a long time on my desk beneath my computer screen like a baby waiting to be named. My natural history guide to the Poconos informed me that there is a series of rubble pits like the one I hiked to all along route 209 between Raymondskill Creek and the town of Milford, just north of where I had made my discovery. The rubble pits, the book said, are full of Devonian fossils. I looked up the word Devonian and found, to my delight, that it refers to a period in Earth's history about 345 million years ago. That is 342 million years before Lucy walked the earth, and still 200 million years before dinosaurs reigned, which already, in itself, seems like a very long time ago.

The Devonian period was a sort of Age of Exploration for the wildlife at the time. For it was then, through that prodding mechanism of natural selection—which caused hominids, in their time, to begin walking upright—that many animals finally took one incredible step—or leap—from saltwater to freshwater or from water onto land. Clams and mussels moved from the warm, inland seas to freshwater ponds and marshes. Scorpions and millipedes developed breathing tubes and inhabited land along with ferns and my absolute favorite: the amphibians.

Turning the fossil over in my hands, I studied its dark, extremely fine grain, its fragile, muddy feel. I figured it was black shale and read that the blacker the shale, the more organic the material it was formed from. Shale consists of clay-sized particles deposited only by very slow-moving streams or larger, still bodies of water—such as warm, shallow, inland seas. The brown and red areas on my fossil most likely indicated that the rock contained oxidized iron. And finally, I was struck by a tiny picture in my Audubon guide of a hillside whose black shale had broken like glass, leaving layers upon layers of windows to an earlier time, opaque, but not unintelligible. Slaty shale the caption said, which, I read further, occurs when heat and pressure realign the particles in the shale and make them harder and more brittle, and I knew it was upon this that I stood.

Lucy's controversy goes beyond her current travel, beyond her initial evidence that humans traveled on foot before becoming smarter. Though it's clear from the angle of Lucy's femur, her locking knee joint, the curvature of her spine, that she was bipedal, her long arms and curved fingers indicate that she still spent time in the trees as well.

In "Climbing to the Top: A Personal Memoir of *Australopithecus afarensis*," J.T. Stern includes two illustrations. The first, a 1972 artist's rendition for Time Life, shows *Australopithecus afarensis*—Lucy and her imagined compatriots—standing and squatting on the savannah next to a watering hole. There are zebras grazing behind them and a small, deer-like animal nearby, and in the distance a few isolated trees. The depiction, with the exception of the fur and facial features of the apes, is eerily reminiscent of pictures of the Garden of Eden. In contrast, in the article's second picture—a 1997 National Geographic drawing of *Australopithecus afarensis*—the ground isn't even visible. The apes are perched on branches in dense, leafy forest. One ape has its right hand wrapped around vines, its left reaching for some high-up, grape-like fruit.

In the earlier illustration, it seems the apes are only an instant away from picking up a rock to crush a seed or throw at a scurrying mammal, that momentarily they'll be dreaming up the religion the picture seems to mimic. Surely becoming human was so profound it happened in an instant, a stroke of evolutionary genius. But since the discovery of Lucy, older fossils have been found which reveal that humans were walking upright for at least a million years before Lucy was. Now, we imagine Lucy as a mosaic—mostly arboreal from the waist up, mostly bipedal from the waist down. She was a combination of past and future in a prolonged present, an uncertain work in progress, from our perspective an artful swinger with an awkward gait.

During the time when I thought I would never be able to properly identify Fatso, I returned home for a holiday and found, to my surprise, that my father had either exaggerated or I had misunderstood: Fatso was still there between the port-o-potty and a new gravel driveway that now runs along and then veers off of Swingset Road. Most of Swingset Road, I found, isn't even on our property, but luckily our swingset was—or at least, the new swingset my parents had bought for my sisters' children. The whole family went out to inspect the foundation for the new house being built next door; someone had placed a wooden stick with orange flagging next to the rock that we always knew (but never cared) marked the end of our property. We walked past it and there Fatso was, in pieces: a trunk about ten feet long, uprooted and dragged to the side of the pit left when they pulled him from the ground. Covering the pit were several of his large branches in a pile with the much smaller trunks of cherries and birches.

Fatso had thrown up some new shoots and I quickly began the routine of identification, grateful for that one last chance: he had opposite branching, smooth, green, round twigs, and pale yellow sapwood beneath his stretched outer covering. Next to where he stood, spared, grew a tree about eight inches in diameter with a clear pattern of diamonds in its bark. While I was pondering this and committing the information to memory—failing, for some reason, to take samples for verification or as keepsakes—someone pointed out a vine on the spared tree. My father ran for his pruning saw to cut off the bottom so that his grandchildren could swing on it. In five minutes the work was done and someone else lifted a nephew high in the air to grab onto the vine and pulled him by the ankles and let go. The boy swung back and forth, back and forth, his face smug and the family watched—silent, complacent, afraid—until he jumped off, instinctively, at the top of the arc and landed deftly on his feet. He was six years old.

When Lucy chose to walk, rather than swing, around her environment, she experienced even more benefits than just having hands free for creating and using tools. Her food supply increased; she could gather nourishment not only from high in the trees, but also from bushes and low branches. While she was doing so, she could see predators over tall grass. And because she could stand upright, she likely experienced reduced skin exposure to the sun and increased cooling by wind evaporation. At first, it seems, the adaptation of bipedalism was a boon, but on this earth—and this is my worry—change can lead as easily to extinction as to proliferation.

Travel is risky. Bipedalism requires a narrower pelvis, which decreases the size of the canal through which a newborn baby must pass. Brain sizes began to increase in ancient humans about two million years ago, with a major expansion occurring 500,000 years ago and modern proportions reached 350,000 years later. The combined result of bipedalism and large brains relative to body size—the two features which distinguish humans from other primates—is that human childbirth is extremely complex, dangerous, and painful.

Compared to other animals, human infants have a relatively short gestational period and a resultant long time to maturity: they are born with their brain only 25% developed. Human labor can take up to twenty-four hours; chimpanzees, our closest living relatives, normally labor only for one or two. Human infants must navigate the birth canal with special twists and turns because they can only fit through facing away from their mothers, with their noses toward the mother's perineum. This makes it nearly impossible for mother and baby to survive birth unassisted. In chimpanzees, which have wider pelvises, thus allowing babies to be born facing forward, the mother chimp can reach down and pull the baby up along her stomach, causing its body to bend along the natural flex of the spine. If a human mother tries to catch her own baby, who is born facing backward, she risks breaking its neck and withholding it from travel forever by paralyzing it.

Lucy arrived safely in Houston, and has moved on for exhibit at other institutions, but the argument surrounding her travel still rages. With the exception of her impromptu display on the airport table by her finder, Johanson, Lucy has been displayed to the public only briefly twice before, in her home country. She's spent the far greater part of the last four decades in climate-controlled vaults, only brought out for study by scientists.

The Smithsonian Institute and the New York Museum of Natural History have refused to participate in Lucy's U.S. tour. They fear for Lucy's survival. Johansan, however, has admitted that standing before Lucy's actual bones, rather than a model, will produce psychological benefits in admirers that may be well worth the risk. Seeing the true matter of our ancient, bipedal ancestor, we will be more accepting of the theory of evolution, of the human's position in earth's systems, of our indebtedness to nature and our obligation to preserve it and, along with it, ourselves. Whatever the outcome, like it or not, Lucy is once again on the move; she will be traveling for the next six years before returning home.

After I found it, I tried to identify my fossil for a long time, tried to reconstruct in animal form the shape the black shale had taken. I wished for it to be a trilobite, something that sounds very old and exciting and that is no longer found in the current species record, for even though their numbers were in decline during the Devonian, the largest trilobites ever alive occurred at that time. But after a few weeks of careful examination and some chipping away, instead I saw a pair of bivalves—two simple mussels—though I was never really certain. I returned to the outcrop of slaty shale where I found the fossil and tried to imagine I was standing in what was once there, what always sounds so inviting to me: the warm inland seas that existed at that time, and I was over-whelmed by what was nameless in my life—what was recent and ancient, and what was nearly gone forever.

Fatso is a white ash. Although science theorizes that ash may be one of the most recently evolved tree species, in Norse mythology, ash is ancient. Ash was the tree that supported the entire universe, the tree from which man and woman were created. It is the tree that will harbor and nourish and re-produce man and woman when the day of reckoning comes. The ash that held up my family is gone, but, as the myth predicts, there is a vine on a smaller ash that my descendants have swung upon.

In Pennsylvania, I stood hundreds of miles from where I climbed Fatso. I was finally off the map, unreachable by Doghouse or Swingset Road. I knew that I had not gone as far as I would go—there would be other opportunities in many other places, the creation of my own children to pursue. But I felt always that I must return, like the frogs that called from their wetland perches, as if I could not set down roots out of the water, or, like Lucy, out of the forest. I was not ready, and yet I was heading out. The sea was knocking at my knees, making it difficult to stay put, but the clay beneath grasped at my feet. Space and time came together again, and I listened for a prophecy, my mother's voice directing me toward profit and security. But on this point, she was quiet. I did not know—and I still do not know—where the risk lay for that first amphibian, for Lucy then and now, and for me: if staying means I will remain, or if I will disappear by leaving.

PART III

Subimago

[10] *Clues*

I could never imagine the ruins of May Utz's house without their surrounding web of brush and trees. My sisters and I could not fathom a lawn, or a path to her garden. We knew the ruins meant that this place had once been a home, that at one time the house had stood up from the ground like our own, taming the area immediately around it, but we could not erase the forest which had taken over since May Utz had moved.

A few dozen yards from the ruins was a spring. A long time ago, someone had built a concave, hip-high wall of fieldstone into the hill behind and above where the water began to seep, creating a place where the water could collect and stream from. We viewed this as a place to spot minnows, frogs, and salamanders, another path to the creek, and not a woman's nearest source of water in the early twentieth century.

On our way to the creek we would stop to pick phlox, bluebells, and daffodils. These flowers came up beneath an under-story, within a shrub layer, that forced us to walk doubled-over even at school-age height. Somewhere in our minds we knew these hard, bold flowers were garden varieties, descendants of the road and the house, survivors, but I liked to imagine them—as I liked to imagine us—as wild.

We were not supposed to explore the house, but we had to pass by May Utz's to get to the creek, which was in our dominion. The house's remoteness, something that always puzzled us, was really the result of how we approached it: through our woods on paths that we had made, into a long cornfield that began to lead down, and then into a thicker woods that led vaguely and more steeply and without paths. Suddenly we would find ourselves stepping off of a stone wall we hadn't known we'd been on; the wall sided a curve in an old woods road that seemed to just appear out of nowhere. We walked along it for a while to get to the creek, where the road opened up and just stopped. But in the other direction we never went farther than the spring, and so in our minds the road stopped there also, and had no beginning. It didn't make sense—this piece of road dropped next to a pile of someone's home. It felt placed, or misplaced, rather than overgrown.

According to my father, his grandmother's family called this road, in its entirety, "the Old Dug Road," but as I remember it, the Old Dug Road was not dirt. It was covered with grass. One of our neighbors kept it mowed, my father says, but to us it was just naturally the way it was—a place for grass to grow to a certain height, and then stop. Across from the curve in the road, nearly hidden in the brush, was May Utz's house.

The house looked as if it had been stepped on. The

roof was on the ground, and concealed the remains of any windows or walls. It was so unreal, in the middle of the most distant place we could carry ourselves to at that age without bikes, that whenever I would jump from the wall onto the Old Dug Road I almost expected to see the feet of a witch sticking out from under it. On the side was a cold rectangle of forest floor that opened and led to the root cellar. We explored it many times. I don't remember what we found— maybe jars of canned foods—only that it was full. We were looking, I think, for what my toddler nephew fills the trunk of his tricycle with when my husband takes him around the block when we visit his family in Milwaukee: clues. A stick, a piece of litter, whatever catches his eye goes into the yellow plastic trunk. "Clues," he says when the two of them return, and he points to each thing he has collected, and we know what he means, for we grew up too in search of something, in search of what we would inhabit, and how we would fill our lives.

In the middle of July, in Stevens Point, Wisconsin, where I live now, the sun rises at 5:27 am and sets at 8:41 pm, resulting in 15 hours and 14 minutes of this particular location's portion of about one two-billionth of the sun's total radiation, the amount of radiation the entire earth is receiving at any given time. On that same day, in Finksburg, Maryland, where May Utz lived before she died, and where I used to live, the sun will rise at approximately 5:40 am and set at 8:38 pm, resulting in 14 hours and 58 minutes of sunlight. This is still a long summer day, but more than a quarter hour shorter than a long summer day in Wisconsin. It may not seem like much, but when I moved here, combined with the level horizon and the open fields, I felt this increase in the amount of sunlight right away.

And I take it greedily—this quarter hour—without remorse, or consideration. I let it lap over me at the edges of what I perceive to be too many lakes. I let it sit on my shoulders while I pass the lakes in search of winding creeks like the one that drew my sisters and I by May Utz's so many years ago once or twice a week. I let it burn the part in my hair as I cleave through fields, searching for what I am used to: a filter of trees that will segment the light, send it in long, slanted, parallel streams that reveal the rising and falling of forest dust, a kind of warm breathing. I take it sometimes in the morning, but more often after chores at noon, or in the evening, when it lingers and I linger with it. It is the first thing from this place that I have willingly received.

On any given day in my youth, if we weren't traipsing by May Utz's abandoned one in the woods, my sisters and I might have been designing our own little homes. We created them with a mixture of plastic and wooden toy furniture on the surfaces of our own personal footstools. My oldest sister's footstool was painted black, my middle sister's was a kind of dull, bird's-egg blue, and mine red. We used wooden alphabet blocks as stairs, and divided up the furniture and characters. Most of the time was spent in setting up the homes, the elaborate second floor rooms we designed on the surfaces of the stools. The game was all about building homes. It rarely lasted long enough to play at living in them.

During the time that we were regularly passing by the ruins of her old home in the bottom by the creek, May Utz was living in a sagging, two-story, four-room house up on the ridge, right on our street. I don't know who she was or what she looked like. When I ask my parents about her, they give me a numbered list of ten things. The list includes a son named Gilbert, how many acres of land May Utz owned, even that she may have been related to a great-aunt of ours.

I came to know May Utz the most not from this recent research, but when I first learned to write. For it was then May Utz became more human, this woman whose former home seemed to have been lowered from above into the woods where I played, placed without access to anything. When I learned to write, I could finally see the sounds that made up her name instead of just hearing them. It seems she was never the subject of a sentence, as in "May Utz lived there"—or lives here for that matter—but always she showed possession: "That house was May Utz's," or "We were down by May Utz's." As a result, her names had run together in the voice of my father, the one who had walked us past her abandoned house in the first place, to form a single noun, something that sounded like a disease—mayootsis—an abnormal condition of the mind or body that I could only imagine.

I was born at 39.29 degrees north and 76.53 degrees west. I have lived at 41.15 degrees north, 74.75 degrees west;41.44 degrees north, 74.01 degrees west, and 41.23 degrees north, 75 degrees west. Now I live at 44.52 degrees north, 89.58 degrees west.

Before my husband and I moved, I would often wake in the night from an unrelated dream. My eyes would pop open, and suddenly I could feel them like globes; I could see the magnitude of what we were about to do, our proposed trajectory 800 miles across the planet, about one-thirtieth of the way around the world.

May Utz's was not the only abandoned home that I remember coming across in my childhood. There was another I discovered once, by accident, alone. This one was also in the bottom, but on the other side of the ridge, near the east branch of the creek, which would join up with the west branch, the one by May Utz's, in Patapsco, where my grandmother lived.

I was following the river when I found, wound in brambles that were dotted with the blood-red of male cardinals, this barely approachable abandoned house. It was still standing, so I entered it. Like May Utz's basement, it was amassed with stuff: stacks of paper, sofas, pots, mirrors, tools, dolls. What I remember most, I found after creeping carefully up the stairs to the second floor. There, I lifted down a heavy cardboard box from the top of a closet that was clearly and decisively labeled "ice skates that do not fit."

I knew the move to my new home would be hard. Thirteen degrees west in longitude translates to about eight hundred miles, seventeen hours in a car, two in a plane. And before it happened, my internal GPS used to knock me awake at night and it was as if I had already stepped off the planet. I could see the dark sphere of earth and where I had lived and where I was going and yet I was viewing it from somewhere else in the solar system. In the moments before waking, in the dark, I could feel the distance. In the morning, in the light, I couldn't see how far it really was.

What I didn't expect was how different five more degrees north would feel. And it's not that it's colder, but something else. I had already moved around a bit in recent years, but with this move, I was so focused on the twelve degrees west, I hadn't considered the little hop north and what might be its effects. The summer I arrived I thought I had gained time. All I could see was sky with no interruption of trees and a sun that seemed to idle. The days felt longer and they were longer. On the summer solstice, the sun rose for me in Wisconsin at 5:13 am and set at 8:46 pm, offering a full fifteen hours and twenty-three minutes of sunlight. It was the longest day of the year, and, so far, the longest day of my life.

The second day after I met my husband at school in New Jersey, I invited him along for a hike on the Appalachian Trail. We went off trail looking for an Indian fault cave that was not on the map but mentioned in our guidebook. Instead, we found an abandoned house in the woods. Like May Utz's basement, and the house along the east branch of the Patapsco River, this house was still full of the family's things: furniture, catalogues, a refrigerator. We decided it was important that we each take something, so we tiptoed in and took two vases. One of them ended up becoming a code between us, a dowry we passed back and forth before negotiating a relationship; I'd leave the room at a party and when I returned the narrow vase would be in my drink; the next morning before he left to catch a plane for a weekend back home in Wisconsin, he'd find it on his windshield.

In mid-November, according to my chart, the sun does not rise in Stevens Point until 6:56 am, and it sets at 4:30 pm, resulting in just nine hours and thirty-six minutes of sunlight. This is nearly a full six hours shorter than a day just five months before it. But worse somehow is the comparison I make to the mid-November days where I grew up, which are still occurring, at 39.29 degrees north, 76.53 degrees west, without me: there the sun rose at 6:58 am and did not set until 4:49 pm, giving nearly ten hours of sunlight, a full fifteen minutes more than I am currently getting.

But the first clue I picked up in Wisconsin is a hoax. For the total number of hours of daylight is the same whatever your latitude. Wherever you are on the planet, over the course of one year, you receive an average of twelve hours of light per day; you spend about 50% of your time in the light, and the other half out of it. No one collects more of anything. I have out here as much sunlight as I had in Maryland; it's just that it was doled out more evenly there from season to season. From this point on in my life, the days will be simply be longer in summer and shorter in winter than I am used to.

My husband and I began to look for a home to buy at 41.23 degrees north, 76.53 degrees west, in Pennsylvania, near where we worked in New Jersey. One of our requirements: we wanted a basement, not easy to come by in that region, because they have to be dug out of the rocky Pocono plateau. In one newly-built home, the ground floor had been completely inundated with snow-melt, which then refroze. We stood at the garage door, which opened at the back into the basement, trying to balance on several inches of ice that had turned the entire floor from wall to wall into a skating rink. Even if something like this never happened again—as the realtor promised with a surprisingly straight face—we knew we would never be able to visualize the basement as anything other than a winter pond.

To see another home, we had to sign forms stating that we knew the house was dangerous, but that we chose to enter anyway: there the walls were covered with molds and fungus set down on the paneling instead of the forest floor where they belonged. After this, we moved our search to Wisconsin, following a job, and my husband's desire to move back to the state of his birth and his childhood.

Before we signed the offer on our first home here we wrote clearly the following stipulation: we wanted everything out of it. Everything, we stressed to the realtor, but as we showed our relatives pictures of our new conquest, they shook their heads: holiday decorations sat on exposed insulation in the unconverted attic, bank records from thirty years ago clogged the barn—shoeboxes upon shoeboxes of returned checks.

But the night we moved in, we were impressed: everything was gone. We vacuumed and set up our bed. The next day we moved in all the furniture we had acquired from a series of small apartments, and the house was still empty. After three years, we have yet to fill all its rooms.

After May Utz died, I went into her second house—the one up on the ridge. The one in the valley next to the creek was unreachable; our woods and the cornfield behind it had become lawns for new homes, and although the land was never ours to begin with, to walk it at that point, as adults over cut grass, would be more like trespassing. But May Utz's sagging second home, the one on our street, I snuck up behind one day—perhaps lured by the wineberries that lined her woods—and entered through a back door. There was no bathroom, and its evenness of two second floor rooms stacked on top of two ground floor rooms reminded me of the symmetrical houses that we had built, as children, on our footstools.

On the list of ten things about May Utz my mother had written, "It was said that there was only a path to walk through in her house—it was so junky. This was in her old age." And it is true—one of the many things I found that day was a cluster of half-full prescription bottles of something or other on a narrow shelf. I used to wonder, as I pored over what these houses contained, about the circumstances of their disposal. In each of these abandoned houses it was as if there had been a war, as if the family had been suddenly plucked out, not able to take anything. It was odd to have a surplus of ice skates, for instance, but more peculiar was what would cause the type of person who had such an organized way of maintaining such a thing to one day just up and leave it.

As I explored them, I wondered about the moment when each house became empty of life, the last time someone exited a door, the decision that nothing was salvageable, nothing was of worth. And I searched for clues—an old coin that would positively date things, a human bone, family jewelry. Whatever I found, I now realize—extra winter sports equipment, a cheap vase, half of an unused prescription—was just as important. What these homes held was normal. They showed a natural progression of acquiring, gathering, storing.

Beneath our house there is a cistern that my husband found by crawling up from the basement into a narrow earthy passage below the kitchen. On our stomachs, one day, we go in together, and he shows me. The ground is orange and sandy, with some litter in the corners. I still cannot subdue that desire to look for clues. But I am immobilized, sandwiched between the earth and the floor of our home, waiting for what my husband wants to show me. He needs my help to lift up a sheet of plastic. Then he tugs at a surface of tightly fitted wooden planks beneath. One comes up. The sunlight does not reach here, so he shines the flashlight down into a basin neither of us knew was there, that we have walked above without echo for almost a year. I stare at a thin pipe that pierces the air midway down, the other end of which I imagine led to a gutter on the roof that funneled a day's rain inside, or to a hand pump in the kitchen that once filled a family's bowls, and I can't help but think—what will we leave behind? For it is deep as a man and dry as a bone.

[11] My Own Little Mass Extinction

When our pet hermit crab died, my sisters and I put its body in a small, red-white-and-blue box that had once held a roll of caps for our cap gun. We gave it a proper burial between the woods and our yard. But after a month's time, I became curious about what had happened to the hermit crab's body underground, so I dug it up. The dead crab slid out soft and supple, more receptive to my touch than it had ever been while alive; its segmented legs, probably water-logged, seemed to cuddle with my palm. Before I could really begin my inspection, however, I was caught.

My older sisters stood on the grass and gaped, too shocked to come near. They threw out warnings about vengeance and ghosts, then continued on their way, wanting no part in it. Squatting there, age seven or eight, with the soggy cap-box at my side and the limp crustacean in my palm, I had an odd, conscious moment of cultural awakening. I suddenly realized I had committed something worse than murder. To kill is sometimes unethical, and sometimes not, but to play with the dead is always perverse.

Many years later I would apply for some type of environmental position which required the ability to commit murder. Getting right to the point, the first question the interviewers asked was, Can you kill Raccoons? People always bring them in, they said, orphaned babies, families who've made nests in their chimneys. I replied, Yes, because I knew it was the right answer. I agreed that euthanization was the best option for nuisance animals from a species that was doing quite well in today's human-altered world, and furthermore, was infamous for spreading rabies. This is what I knew at the time: that it is ridiculous to save individual animals when what is suffering is the whole earth. It's a good thing I didn't get that job because in spite of my brief childhood foray into the post-mortem world, I know now that I cannot end an animal's suffering if it means I have to kill it and watch it die myself.

Aside from recent natural and unnatural deaths of hermit crabs and raccoons, Earth has been through five major mass extinctions of its plant and animal species since life began. A mass extinction occurs when large proportions of the earth's biota die off in a period of time that is relatively short. The first known mass extinction was 440 million years ago and the most recent was 65 million years ago. All of these extinctions have been the result of major physical changes on the planet, largely climate changes caused by plate tectonics, volcanoes, collisions with asteroids, or glaciation. Scientists like to point out that 99.9% of all the species that have ever existed are now extinct. That's almost everything. Extinction is hardly something new; extinction is a part of life on Earth.

Many scientists believe we are currently in the midst of a sixth mass extinction, one that will rival the most severe mass extinction in history, which occurred at the end of the Permian period, 245 million years ago, and resulted in the loss of 90% of the animal species in existence at that time. Although the numbers are just estimates, and the estimates vary from scientist to scientist, some scientists list our current loss of species at seventy times what is known as the background extinction rate—what the extinction rate reasonably should be.

Uniquely, the cause for this sixth mass extinction is not physical. It is, as paleontologist Niles Eldredge puts it, biotic. In other words, Earth's species are disappearing today at the sometimes-estimated rate of three per hour solely because of one of Earth's own living creations—*Homo sapiens sapiens*.

After a couple weeks' vacation, I return to my home in Wisconsin to tend to my garden. My new border collie pup, Betsy, who is having trouble remaining within our property lines—she likes to run off into the surrounding fields of corn and soybeans on several-hour solo jaunts—accompanies me outside. I've lived in this state, which my husband is from, for just a year, in this house for just six months, but with my garden and my dog, and hopefully, soon, a child, I am trying to establish my life here, eight hundred miles from where I was born and grew up. I am trying to make it seem like home.

In the garden, I'm pleased to find, the pumpkins seem to have taken over just as much as the weeds; I'm standing in a miniature jungle. It's my fault the garden looks this way: as a first time planter, I didn't have any faith. When the seeds I planted came up late and spindly, I went to the store and bought the tallest, most robust-looking greenhouse-grown plants I could find. It felt a bit like cheating, but I was worried my earlier plantings would produce nothing. I put these new plants in between my rows of weak shoots. As the seed packets advised, I had already planted double what I wanted of everything because I knew they would not all survive and that later, just like the bodiless hand pictured on the packet that pulled up the sparest-looking sprouts, I would thin them. But suddenly everything began looking healthy—both seeds and bought plants—and I couldn't "thin" anything, a word that seemed to me, akin to murder. So now I have three times the garden I intended.

I am pulling up handfuls of hip-high grasses, which my pumpkins and cucumbers refuse to cease embracing, in an attempt to reveal my strawberry plants, which appear to have been doing quite well without me in the shade of these weeds. I notice with content that Betsy is still in the yard. But then I see that she seems to be having a peculiarly good time over by the barn. Her tail is high and wagging. She rolls in the grass, rubs her neck on the ground. Then she picks up something large and floppy and throws it into the air. When it falls, she rolls on top of it.

Grabbing my zip-loc baggy of bacon strips, I mosey over to find out what is going on. Betsy throws the object into the air again, and I see that it is a baby rabbit. It is her first catch. In an attempt to save the rabbit by diverting her attention, I dump out the entire bag of treats on the ground behind me. Just as I wished, Betsy leaps over to consume the bacon strips, leaving behind her trophy.

The rabbit is badly mangled in the rear, with baby squash-like organs protruding, but it is still breathing. I know what I have to do, and I start thinking about where I might find a broom, calculating the time it will take me to run to the tool shed to get one against the rate at which Betsy is eating the treats and will thus finish and return to her original feast. Then I notice what appears to be an old fence post, a stout log lying a few feet away in the grass. It almost seems to have been put there just for my intended purpose—as if I were being tested and some overseeing god was supplying me with tools to lure me one way or the other.

Aside from my theoretical response to that single job interview question, this is the first time in my life I have been presented with the task of killing something other than an insect. My grandmother used to kill chickens for dinner, and my mother has described the scene for me, but I am two generations removed from having to kill my own food, and one generation removed from even witnessing it.

So I pick up the log with great effort and, in a kind of split-personality moment, scream "No!" through real tears, as if to stop myself, each time I hit the suffering animal. The rabbit squeals in agreement. Suddenly Betsy arrives at my side, finished with her feast, and snatches up the now perished rabbit between hits. She runs across the yard, flings it into the air, nudges it with her nose, (wondering why it won't hop), rolls in it, then picks it up and flings it again. I wonder what kind of look, what kind of warning—like the one my sisters gave me—I can give to this dog to get her to stop what she's doing.

Somehow I catch up with her. I can't really let her eat the dead rabbit. She might choke on a bone—as all the dog-training books warn—or she could get worms. Out of treats, I put my hands around her jaws and begin to pry them open, gradually moving to the tips for better leverage. Eventually she gives in and lets the carcass go. I snatch up the rabbit, walk to the trash can, and throw it in on top of the bags, staring at the corpse for a moment to make sure it is dead before I close the lid.

Betsy's catch could have been any one of three species, I am surprised to find, in the state I now live in. In the Mid-Atlantic, where I moved from about a year ago, we had only the Eastern cottontail. But out here, the family Leporidae is represented by the Eastern cottontail rabbit as well as two hares, the jackrabbit and the snowshoe. Hares, usually larger with longer hind legs than rabbits, also differ in that they are born fully furred and with their eyes open. The young have a special name: leverets. The fur of hares turns white in winter. They generally hang out alone, whereas bunnies, or baby rabbits, are born furless, with closed eyes, in a depression in the ground lined with soft grass and fur which the mother plucks from her own body. They often hang out together, even as adults.

Wisconsin has a plethora of small mammals to which I am not accustomed. My husband narrowly misses something with his car, and in the rear-view mirror it looks like a short, fat weasel crossing low to the road, not a vole, not a squirrel, nothing either of us has ever seen before. I decide later it was a Franklin's ground squirrel, or gray gopher. I can't really be sure—this squirrel is actually listed as imperiled in Wisconsin. It is only moderately likely to be seen in my county, due to a loss of its grassy habitat from agriculture, road construction, urbanization, and forest succession. Still, I am delighted that out here I have so many new animals to choose from: the thirteen lined ground squirrel, Eastern fox squirrel, and the least chipmunk, to name a few.

In the time it takes me to dispose of the first dead rabbit—or hare—in the trashcan, Betsy has caught another one, in an entirely different corner of the yard. I can see that this one is still very much alive, for it is inadvertently playing with her, jumping and squealing while she paws at it in an almost human way. Without anymore bacon strips to trick her with, I am unsuccessful in retrieving it; every time I get within two feet of Betsy, she grabs her prize and runs a half-circle away.

Not wanting to have to partake in a second murder, I need to get to the rabbit before it is too badly injured. I go in the house and grab a hotdog from the freezer. Regardless of the fact that my dog is currently sucking the blood of a half-live rabbit, I microwave the hotdog for one minute—as the dog-owner guidebooks have informed me to do, to make sure it is safe to eat—and run back outside. Betsy is lying in the yard with the rabbit in her mouth. It is not moving.

I hold out the hot dog and Betsy's head and ears perk up. The head and back legs of the rabbit, extending from the sides of her mouth, droop lower. She has never had an entire hotdog before, only snippets stuffed with antibiotics or tiny pieces for sitting and lying down on command at obedience class. Slowly the rabbit slides to the ground. I toss the hotdog to the right with one hand and reach for the rabbit with the other. I can now see that the rabbit is very much alive. This time I don't need a broom or a fencepost, but a box.

To get away from Betsy, I take the rabbit in the house. Unable to find a box, I go to the pantry and grab a paper grocery bag and drop it inside. Immediately I hear the rabbit's claws scratching at the bottom of the bag, a good sign. I fold over the top so it cannot jump out, although it is only the size of one of my hands and probably cannot jump that high—unless it is a hare rather than a rabbit, which are generally jumpers instead of runners, at least when escaping predators.

Betsy, finished with the hotdog, is waiting at the door. I open it, and when she smells the bag of rabbit she jumps into the house. Ducking outside, I leave her stranded in the kitchen, then go to the porch and sit the paper bag down to decide what to do.

I am still wearing my garden gloves, so I reach in and pick up the baby rabbit. What has always looked drab brown to me when glimpsed in the headlights of my car, here in my hands, is surprisingly colorful. It is a much deeper brown, almost black, and flecked with cream and red. In spite of the situation, I am suddenly like that unselfconscious child again, digging up the dead hermit crab at the edge of her woods. I am curious, and thankful for this opportunity for a close-up view of one of the wild inhabitants of my yard. I am about to decide exactly what kind of Leporidae it is when I notice the rabbit has a hole in one of its legs. By hole, I mean I can see bone, although there is no blood. Also, his tail is folded underneath him and feels broken. He begins to tremble.

I put him down on the ground to further diagnose his

condition. He begins to hop, and before I know it, he has hopped under the porch and away from me, to a place where, if I let Betsy out within the next twenty-four hours she can squeeze in and catch him, and if I do not, I realize, he will probably die from internal hemorrhaging and we will all be smelling him in a few days. I take off the gardening gloves and go in the house to join Betsy.

That evening Betsy catches a mouse in the burn pile out back, a pit which is now a mound of weeds, in which the previous owners of the house burned most of their trash instead of taking it to the landfill. The mouse is dead by the time I get to Betsy. Like a pro I pull it by the tail out of her mouth and carry it into the house and all the way upstairs to show my husband, wanting, somehow, to make him an accomplice to these murders. Then I dispose of it, dropping it into the trash next to the deceased rabbit.

The next day, I return to the garden to finish weeding. When I step over the low fence, which is about two feet high, I see, lying right at the corner, between my first two strawberry plants, a dead baby rabbit.

I have not had a problem with rabbits—or anything, for that matter—in this garden all season. I have not had to set out mothballs, pee around the perimeter, tie tin pans to blow in the wind, or make a scarecrow. Nothing has been nibbled or half-eaten. Nothing has gotten in. Nothing living, that is.

Although the garden is a clear one hundred yards of open lawn from the porch, I assume it is the broken-tailed rabbit with the hole in its leg from yesterday. Injured as it was, I don't know how the rabbit made it across that great expanse and up over the fence. I can't help but feel that the rabbit has been placed here, in this deliberate corner, like a message on a doorstep. As if these two things, paired—my modest garden and my poaching puppy—foretold of some greater misfortune. I want to pick it up and check for the tooth-hole in the right rear leg, the broken tail, but I'm not willing to get dead rabbit all over a second pair of gardening gloves. I leave it there to show my husband.

Niles Eldredge, the paleontologist who has poignantly marked the current mass extinction as biotic in cause rather than physical, is curator-in-chief of the "Hall of Biodiversity" at the American Museum of Natural History and author of Life in the Balance: Humanity and the Biodiversity Crisis. Eldredge gives two reasons for the mass extinction he sees happening on Earth at the moment, both of which I have taken part in, in my own small way, in my lifetime: the dispersal of hunting-gathering humans from Africa to various parts of the world beginning about 100,000 years ago, and more recently, about 8,000 B.C.E, the advent of agriculture.

Wherever humans migrated, he and other scientists point out, and the fossil record supports, large game species became extinct soon after. Man hit Australia about 60-50,0000 years ago. Australia's mass extinction began, accordingly, 4,000 or so years later with the loss of things we can barely imagine: the giant kangaroo; thylacoleo, the marsupial lion; diprotodon, a mammal that looked like a cow-sized wombat; a giant flightless bird; and a 26 foot lizard. Humans crossed from Siberia to North America about 12 to 13,000 years ago, and within just about a thousand years, this continent lost, among others, mastodons, giant ground sloths, giant beaver, and saber-tooth cats. There is debate on just how humans disrupted these local ecosystems, whether it was direct, through overhunting, or indirect, through disease. Whatever the cause, more and more it is agreed that the migration of hunting and gathering humans was contemporaneous with mass extinction.

Beginning about 8,000 years ago, and much worse for the earth even, according to Eldredge, humans began to do more than just eradicate things; they began to manipulate them. They did this through simple gardening, which quickly grew into full-fledged agriculture. Now humans can reduce diverse local ecosystems to monocultures of one or two genetically homogeneous crops, produce corn the size of your arm, much larger than the two-centimeter long cobs that existed naturally 5,000 years ago. And by selective breeding, humans can make cows, pigs, and goats dumber and more docile, and smaller or bigger at will. We then release them to graze, in large numbers, over expanses of natural grasslands. Loss, even extinction, seems somehow understandable, predictable. It happens, as history has shown us. But producing life that contains mostly our desired characteristics—a burpless cucumber, a seedless tomato—seems frivolous, even dangerous.

The day after I find it, I decide I should probably dispose of the dead rabbit that is in the garden. Armed with a folded paper grocery bag to slide under the corpse, I approach the place where, the day before, it was. To my surprise, when I step over the fence and glance down between the two spreading strawberry plants, there is no dead rabbit, only the shape of a dead rabbit in the dust. It looks like someone has sprinkled a mixture of soil and hair into the mold of the profile of a rabbit right between my strawberry plants. When I touch it with a finger, expecting to find guts and gore beneath, there is just dust. One lucky foot does tip up from the dust, but that is all. I am amazed at how quickly and completely the rabbit has decomposed, or vanished.

Within fifteen minutes, Betsy, who has come out again with me, makes her fourth catch. This one is much harder to get from her; it involves fifteen minutes of tag and several tiny, t-bone-steak-flavored treats launched into the air. In fact, I take a break from the tag and fiddle for a while with the sprinkler in my garden, wondering why it won't rotate all the way around, knowing that with each second the rabbit in Betsy's mouth is becoming less and less alive, and thus, that I will be less and less likely to have to kill it myself. I am willing to admit now that this is something I do not want to have to partake in. I certainly don't want another scene like the first day, with the fence post, which I took up in an act to end the rabbit's suffering, a suffering I knew logically the animal did not deserve to endure, but that, in my gut, I really did not want to play a part in stopping.

When I finally get the rabbit, I don't know what to do to get away from Betsy, so, like the wounded rabbit from under the porch, I go to the only place that seems safe. I head for the garden and step over its low fence.

The rabbit sits in my hands. At first glance, he looks uninjured. But then I notice his left rear foot is dangling by a very fine piece of skin. When the rabbit moves the upper part of his hind leg, the dangling foot spins on its thread of skin like the blade of a fan. I consider my options. Perhaps if he were bleeding, or screaming, I could better relate. But he is still, waiting to see what I will do so that he can react.

I could try to find an animal rehabilitator, I reason. With, hopefully, just a broken leg, this rabbit might be a perfect candidate. But rabbits are hardly threatened or endangered. And they are extremely prolific: a pair can produce up to thirty-six young in one breeding season. And in the wild, most rabbits don't live longer than one year anyway, so the death of this rabbit would hardly break any statistics.

When I worked at one nature center, people frequently brought in turtles with cracked shells. One of the other employees was a compassionate young woman who had once tried to raise two baby opossums she had found near a dead mother on the road. She carried them around in her pockets all day, like the mother would have—opossums are North America's only marsupial. She fed the babies milk with an eyedropper, and even stimulated them to excrete, which the mother would have done with her tongue, by rubbing their rear ends with her fingertips. When people brought us injured turtles, this young woman always attempted to glue the turtles' shells back together, which was generally effective as long as the turtles weren't bleeding, which meant that just their shells were cracked, and not the flesh beneath.

But whether they were bleeding or not, I would put the cracked-shell turtles quietly in the woods behind the building, to die their own deaths. Once, a woman brought in a completely healthy turtle. She stood at the door, the turtle in one hand, saying something like, "Here, you better take this." I asked if it had been hit by a car. "No," she replied, "but it was trying to cross the road, and it's just going to attempt it again, and that road is too busy. It would be safer in here." I wanted to say "How about we leave the turtle out where it belongs, and you just stop driving?" Or, "Should we bring the whole forest inside?" But instead I looked at her like she was crazy, and she blinked back at me. That lady and I didn't make sense to one another.

I put the rabbit down. I know that I am not going to call a wildlife rehabilitator since deep down inside I really don't believe in them. I'm bothered by the fact that they make most of the world feel better by treating the symptom, an individual animal that is suffering before our eyes, while we all drive around ignoring—and creating—the problem: mass extinction.

Again, I have the feeling that I really should kill this wounded baby rabbit. Its leg is broken. There is no way it can survive. I worked on a farm once, a small operation which existed mostly for Baltimore-city kids to come and learn about and pet farm animals, and one day I was approached by the owner with the job of getting rid of a duck that had been injured. Although it didn't appear to be suffering, for some reason, the farmer decided that she just couldn't let it stick around. She asked if I would be willing to hold it by the feet and swing its head against a tree. I said no, and suggested they just let it go somewhere in the woods; it would be a nice dinner for a fox or a weasel. They thought that was cruel, and I felt numbly misunderstood. So I watched as one woman put the lame duck in a box and closed the flaps, and the farmer went over it—backwards, not forwards—with the tractor.

Still staring at the dangling foot of the baby rabbit, in a ridiculous instant I don't quite allow to materialize, I start thinking about Popsicle sticks and tape and eyedroppers of milk. Immediately, I shake that out of my head, for it's clear what I should have done. Contrary to my dog-training books, I should have let Betsy kill and eat the rabbit. But Betsy hadn't killed this rabbit, and I wasn't going to eat the rabbit, so I wasn't going to kill it either. And frankly, standing here in the garden in the sun was getting hot and probably making the rabbit even more uncomfortable than it already was. So I took it over to the soybean field, where I figured it was cooler, and I set the rabbit down on the ground. On the other side of the field, several acres away, was a strip of woods. It was like placing a wounded lab rat at the start of a maze built for an elephant. Yet I didn't feel cruel. I simply felt not responsible.

I should have let Betsy kill and eat the rabbit. That would have been the most natural. After all, I have always felt a strange sense of understanding when watching, on The Wild Kingdom, a lion attack and eat a zebra or gazelle. More than the resurrection, which I had been taught about in decades of church, what I saw on The Wild Kingdom was something that made sense to me. If you were killed and incorporated into another living thing before your atoms had a chance to cool off—well, wasn't that the closest thing we had to eternal life?

I wonder later how far the broken-legged baby rabbit made it, or if he moved at all, into the curtain of soy. The hundreds of acres of corn and soybeans that surround my house remind me that thanks to our newfound manipulation of plants and animals, humans have been able to produce food in great excess, allowing us to increase our population at a rate that seems to rival even that of rabbits.

A look at the 2001 world census shows that the earth's population has nearly reached 6.5 billion. The rate of increase does seem to be decreasing, at least in developed countries. Still, there are 6.5 billion of us, and even with a decreasing increase, future projections put world population at 9 billion by 2050.

To put the idea of overpopulation in perspective, I have always used an analogy from Brian Swimme, best known for his book The Universe is a Green Dragon. A habitat has something called a carrying capacity, the number of animals that the land and its resources can sustain over time. If there are too many of a certain kind of animal, that animal will exhaust its food source and much of its population will die out. This allows the food source to make a comeback and both populations to re-regulate themselves to carrying capacity.

Swimme takes the example of the tiger, which is, like the human, another fairly large meat-eating mammal, and which might assume a position similar to ours on the food chain. How many tigers are there currently on the planet? About three thousand. Compare that, Brian Swimme says, to 6.5 billion Homo sapiens. Granted, the current number of tigers on Earth is probably below carrying capacity, due to poaching and habitat destruction. Still, the planet could never handle 6.5 billion tigers. Nor can it, probably, handle 6.5 billion of us.

And even if we could stabilize the population immediately, this would not stop the current threat of a mass extinction. For the developed countries, and the United States in particular, consume many, many more resources than those developing countries that are still adding people to the planet. We consume four times as much oil as the next highest oil-user. We are responsible for the spread of agriculture, the destruction of habitat, the high use of fossil fuels and all their polluting effects; an American's environmental impact is 30 to 50 times that of the average citizen in a developing country.

The next day, over the phone, I tell a friend how I killed that first baby rabbit—a story I have been telling all week, over email, to a stranger I meet at the dog park, to coworkers with whom I rarely talk. It's like a rite of passage I have somehow missed—being the cause of death of another living thing. I tell my friend about how I could barely do it, even though I'd had chicken for dinner the night before, I had fish thawing in the fridge as I beat the rabbit down, and I live up the road from a veal farm without any guilt. She responds that ethically she is still a vegetarian, but that she finds now that she likes the taste of chicken and ground beef. We laugh. Yes, she says, we live in a world of contradictions. And between the two of us it's understood that knowing this somehow makes it okay to be a hypocrite.

The next day I call to make my yearly gynecological appointment, and when I mention my doctor's name, the secretary warns me over the phone: "Just so you know, that doctor does not prescribe birth control." I ask why, having not heard this about my doctor before. "I'm not sure," comes the reply, "but it may be for religious reasons." I get off the phone feeling foggy, like I did with the woman who tried to give me the healthy turtle, trying to protect it by taking it indoors. For I know this doctor will prescribe Chlomid, an ovulation enhancer, because she knows I have been trying to reproduce without success for some time, and she has offered it to me. In my mind, preventing a life that may have been seems not nearly as immoral as causing a life that was not naturally possible, not in the evolutionary projection of things. The latter is weird, in the archaic sense of the word; it's Frankensteinian, like examining a corpse, something I was cured of long ago by my sisters' appalled looks. And it seems risky, dangerous, worse than murder.

At the nature center where I used to release the wounded animals that people would bring to me, we had an exhibit of turtles. We also had an exhibit of mice that, like the rabbits in my yard, were very prolific. One day, we decided to feed some of the mice's newest offspring to our painted turtles. They would love it, we knew, these omnivores who were used to getting reptile flakes and a room temperature casserole of dog food, salad, and strawberries.

But in spite of my ecological understanding of the predator-prey relationship, my almost religious perception of how the proteins and fats in one animal's body could be broken down in the stomach of another, then used to create its own proteins and fats, connecting the deceased again to life, I could not do it. None of us could, for when we held the furless babies by their tails over the water, over the sniffing, open beaks of the turtles, the mice squirmed their warm, pink, closed-eyed bodies up toward our fingertips as close as they could get. The elaborate solution, finally, was for someone to put the mice in a bag and rubber-band it to the exhaust pipe on her car. No matter that this murder was premeditated, and that the death it caused could very well have taken longer than being clawed apart underwater and swallowed in chunks, the person who turned on the ignition of the car was at least five feet away from the babies when they died, and facing in the other direction. Afterward, it was easy to drop the baby mice into the artificial pond for the turtles to retrieve on their own as the carcasses sunk to the bottom. Like the rabbits I left to die under the porch, in the soy-field, the farmer who drove backwards over the lame duck concealed beneath cardboard, in this instance, as humans so often are, we were absolved by distance, by what we did not see, or touch.

And now I'm heading my own little mass extinction. I've broken the two golden rules: I've migrated halfway across the country and planted too large a garden, and my only domesticated animal is happily eradicating species I haven't even identified from my yard. And yet, unable to reproduce, from a fitness perspective, I'm not really competing well in my new home. Like the baby rabbit that turned to dust after a day in my garden, should I take this as a warning?

I've lost the original understanding of death, my natural relationship to it as an animal on Earth. As I child, I tried to regain it by digging up my deceased pet. I learned then that passing away is sacred, but I don't think we can fully believe in the sanctity of death—and thus, the sanctity of life, all life—unless we regularly not only witness death, but cause it, ourselves. In the world I live in, buying boneless chicken breasts whenever I get a craving for chicken parmesan, the only death I will ever take part in is my own. Never mind all the deaths I cause indirectly each day by my overconsumption of natural resources. If death doesn't happen at my hands, it's as if it doesn't happen at all. It can disappear with the trash. I have a high-class notion of having it all figured out on an atomic level—it's all just a transfer of proteins, one long chain of collective consciousness, and yet, vainly, I can't end a baby rabbit's suffering. I know what's wrong with the earth: every day I commit mass murder, but if you asked me to, I couldn't kill a single raccoon.

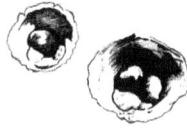

[12] Delicate Baby Dreams

For years, I have dreamed myself a mother. In these dreams I have no memory of conception or birth, and my child, when I finally find it, is fragile and not quite right: a plastic honey container shaped like a bear, emptied of honey and filled with water; some kind of tiny crustacean; a glass bookmark; a bag of cat's eye marbles; a puppy in a bucket in the backyard I can not remember feeding except for some cake on someone's last birthday. I carry the tiny ones around on the fingernail of my pointer finger and try not to blow them away when I exhale. The inanimate ones I hold up to my eyes and ears to scrutinize for any evidence of breathing. I have labeled them "delicate baby dreams," and they come, routinely, with joy and guilt and dissipate with sadness and relief.

Both of my parents had the ability to bring things into being. Some things only my father could find: a place called

Bottle Rock; a particular tree in the forest shaped like a fork; at first, the creek, even; and before that, half of me, when I was unconceived, inside my mother. He knew the best boulder that sloped to the creek's edge and sat at the top while my sisters explored on land or in water and I played in the line of sediment deposited where one met the other. I had a plastic shovel and bucket and was focused on filling it with silt when I tumbled forward into the eddy. The stream could carry me calmly in a straight line to one place, but the beach toys made me think the stream was an ocean that threatened to swallow me whole. I panicked, and my father found me in that too, and delivered me from the creek.

Bottle Rock was a pointed rock on the side of a hill in a nearby woods, named not for what it looked like but for what it contained: a spring. Not a cave, it jutted from the earth as a thick, unshapely roof for an oval pool. From the back of it you could always hear the dark drip of water on water. My sisters and I could never find Bottle Rock on our own, traipsing through the valleys of neighbors' farms, where, alone, we feared being chased by cows, or men who didn't recognize our father in us. Only our father could bring us to this place, to crouch at the dark entrance. This made it seem like Bottle Rock didn't exist without him.

Other acts of creation by my father occurred closer to home, in our own forest. A chestnut oak shaped like a giant fork would magically appear, somehow, after what seemed like hours of searching on our own, when we asked our father to point it out to us. High up the trunk, the tree split into three even brown prongs which were distinct against the sky until you turned and it was gone, and my father was too, back to raking leaves in the yard. It was the same with the statue that marked a neighbor's property line, a stone pylon we knew was visible from the road. Only when our father sprinted a few yards into the woods and touched the top of it did it materialize, the human-stacked stones in the leafy background, beneath the touch of his hand like the tap of a wand. We could only see the forest at that age, I suppose, could not make out in nature these elements of culture—boundaries and tools.

There is a honeybee exhibit that I like to observe at a local nature center, one of those tall, narrow, human-constructed hives where frames of combs are stacked upon one another and covered in Plexiglas, and the bees move in and out of the hive—and the building—by means of a see-through tunnel. Recently, while studying the hive, I watched a honeybee do the waggle dance. I have read about it for years, imitated the dance at summer camps with the preschoolers I've taught. But in this hive I actually saw a bee, almost exactly as described in the encyclopedia, communicating to the other bees, against the wax combs of the hive, where she'd found a good source of nectar.

At first the hive looks like much undifferentiated movement. But if you continue to observe, you will see each of those jobs that you know bees do, but that you barely believe are true, they seem so laden with purpose. There is one depositing nectar into a cell around the periphery of the comb, where the food will be just a short walk to retrieve for a hungry larva, whose wet, white, rice-shaped body squirms among thousands near the hive's protected center. And there is one making honey from the nectar—fanning her wings over a glossy, uncapped cell, evaporating water.

But on this day, amidst the clutter of bees, I saw a sentence being walked over heads and thoraxes and bumped into abdomens and legs. It wasn't as clear to me as to them—and I had needed an interpreter to even be in a position to observe it—still, I saw, and in a sense, heard what one bee was saying.

My mother had the same strange, natural ability to create as my father. I would try it myself, while staring at the portrait of Jesus which hung on the barren walls above the altar of Patapsco United Methodist Church, which my family attended every Sunday. Jesus stood with his arms open against a blue background, and it did seem as if children were coming to him from somewhere outside the picture, just as the stories said, but try as I might, I could never make the children appear. Or, when shopping along Main Street, I would stare at the portrait of J.C. Penney which hung in the old department store. I'd try to envision his name beside his initials. What would I call a son if I had one? For I could . . . John Christopher, Jacob Charles, Jeffrey Carroll. All of them seemed hand-crafted. Perfect.

But nothing was like the only other painting I remember from my childhood: a paint-by-number cat my mother had done—sometime in high school—that sat in the back of her closet. It was brought out once or so each year when one of us bumped into it during a game of hide and seek. I thought it was magnificent, on its black velour background. I couldn't believe how she, a dog-lover, had produced the unmistakable form of this cat from the meager shades of brown and mustard yellow provided in those drugstore kits.

To call it a figure eight is misleading. But that is the human translation, the symbol most often used to describe the motion of a scout bee which has found a promising source of nectar and pollen and wants to lead other bees to it. It is definitely two circles, stacked next to each other. But at times one or the other circle seems more or less complete, and if you focus on finding the eight, the symbol you know, you may miss the point, for both circles seem to be simply a means to get to the run in between, where the bee walks a very important line. If the blossom the scout bee has just visited is opposite the sun, the bee walks straight down the comb; if the blossom is toward the sun, she walks straight up. And of course there are all the exact possibilities in between, on either side. The code is this: the angle the scout bee walks from the pull of gravity is equal to the angle of the source of nectar from the sun.

The waggle dance—called such because the bee wiggles her body during the straight run between the circles—is used only to indicate nectar sources more than thirty-five yards away. Another, simpler dance is used for sources closer. More pieces of the code: in the circling part of the waggle dance, the faster the looping, the closer the supply, and the longer the buzzing during the straight run, the farther away. Also, while the dance is being performed, bees smell and taste the nectar and pollen on the scout bee's body. All this, in the usual darkness of the hive: a dance of sight, touch, smell, taste, and hearing, performed over a jumble of bees, a language that uses all five senses quite precisely to guide and direct to and from, out and home, over and over again.

Now, I can find the eggs of anything: beneath the female crayfish, cupped in the segments of her abdomen, in the hardened foam left by a praying mantis, clasping the woody stem of steeplebush. In grade school a friend and I took the eggs of a mourning dove from her nest beneath a bridge—she had flown away when we approached and so we agreed that they'd been abandoned. But then at school we took them out of their box of cotton and dropped them over the window ledge, first one, and then the other, to our teacher's disbelief and confusion. This, after we realized they weren't going to hatch, that they'd not been adopted, but stolen.

I remember coming upon frogs' eggs at much too late an age—nineteen or twenty. I thought they were something from another planet, these clusters of dark and clear dropped in the water that filled the tire ruts left by an all-terrain-vehicle. But soon they were everywhere, in every pool of water I could find in the forest, and toad's eggs too. I caught the toads hatching in a week; they looked like tiny spiders running from the water to the woods, unless you knelt and noticed they had half the legs, and were in fact jumping.

And there are Red-backed Salamander eggs under every log, like miniature clusters of white grapes, and broad-winged hawk fledglings in a tree at the top of the driveway, and the robin on the porch is on her second brood, and yesterday I nearly touched a fawn with one hand and her sibling with the other, while their mother ate clover on the opposite side of the road, carelessly watching, wondering if I would feed them like someone else must be in the neighborhood.

Though they are nearly all female, just one of the bees in

this hive, and in all hives, is a mother. She is a little bit larger and thinner, more yellow and less striped, and has a straight stinger, unbarbed like her daughters', which she is able to remove from a victim without having to die. But most importantly she has fully developed reproductive organs, and is able to mate and lay eggs. After a single mating, she will lay an egg a minute for her two, three, or four year life, and at will, she will allow that egg to be fertilized or, less often, not, as it passes through her. The fertilized eggs will produce daughters, females without fully developed reproductive organs who will work together to raise her children. The unfertilized eggs, the few hundred or thousand which she will allow over time, will produce drones, or male bees, whose only job is to meet in the forest at predetermined places passed down somehow through generations, and mate with other queens.

Once, I watched a box turtle dig her nest at the top of a hill, clear-cut for telephone poles and electrical lines. It rained, and stopped, and rained again. I had read about how turtles will often abandon several nests before laying and was shocked when her cloaca opened and the leathery, oval-shaped eggs were dropped into the hole before me and covered with dusty earth by her hind legs. I saw more than she did. I marked the nest but didn't check it in any methodical way. Still, a few months later, I came upon the hatchlings digging themselves from the dirt.

My endocrinologist draws me a picture of the pituitary gland on the back of my medical report. The pituitary is a pea-sized gland that hangs in a bony hollow at the base of the brain behind the bridge of the nose, very close to the optic nerve. Only yours, he explains, is plump, shaped like an upside-down lollipop, rather than an upside-down mushroom. You don't have a tumor, another doctor assures. It's probably just how you were made are her exact words. But the lollipop shape restricts my dopamine from inhibiting the production of prolactin—one of the pituitary gland's usual jobs. And the extra prolactin could be affecting the maturing of eggs in my ovaries.

In the Audubon guide to mushrooms, I read about Birds' Nest Fungi. They are tiny cup-shaped mushrooms with seed-like cases shaped like eggs nestled inside. Birds' Nest Fungi are widespread, but are often missed because of their extremely small size; they are only one to three-eighths of an inch high. But of course, within a week, without looking, I have found them, dotting the mulch around the perimeter of the nature center where I go to observe the bees. I raise a bird's nest fungi up to my eyes and inspect its fabrication of miniature eggs. I have no symptoms from my misshapen pituitary gland—my vision feels sharp, almost superhuman, rather than small and distorted. I sit the bird's nest fungi with its egg-mimics down and leave it to await the simple splash of rain that will hit the eggs and release their millions of spores.

When I return to the nature center to look at the bees, most of them are missing. I consult with the summer rangers, and they confirm my suspicions: the hive became too full, and the queen left with half of the worker bees to start a new colony. This means that much has occurred. The workers who stayed behind would have immediately noticed the absence of their queen. They would have selected several larvae at just the right age, and begun feeding them generous amounts of a special substance, royal jelly, that would cause these particular larvae to become fully reproductive female adults. One of the larvae would have metamorphosed early, emerged, and killed the others. And when she was no more than ten days old, this tiny virgin queen would have taken her mating flight.

Because nothing is unseen, I search my book, The ABC and XYZ of Bee Culture, to find out what I have missed. Two scientists, C. Zarlicki and R.A. Morse, fill me in. To observe the mating of honeybees, in 1963, they tied a virgin queen to a very fine thread extending from a helium-filled balloon. In this way, they could follow her to the congregation site of the drones. Once there, they photographed the drones flying behind and slightly below her in what they describe as a "comet-shaped swarm." When the queen's sting chamber and vagina opened wide—how they observed this I am not quite sure—one drone flew straight up from the swarm to join her. As they came together, a loud pop could be heard.

For some reason, I am fixated on the scientists' method. I imagine the balloon to be bright red, the color of a heart, of blood, of a siren, all the more easy to follow. I wonder if it tangled in brambles on the journey or caught the wind and tugged the queen along. For some reason, I don't think the loud pop described in the book, which is never explained, has anything to do with the balloon, but rather with the moment life was created. After the experiment was over, I imagine, perhaps one of the scientists took the red helium-filled balloon home for own his son or daughter, or perhaps, coming from the apiary or the lab, a second loud pop could be heard.

I am in my parents' home and my niece wants to create a picture. I ask for colored pencils and my father tells me without hesitating, "They are downstairs resting on a paint can lid that is sitting on top of a pile of crayons in an Easter basket under your old desk. The paint can lid is to keep the colored pencils from mixing in with the crayons," he explains. I can follow my father's directions to anything, at least in this land, in this house, but elsewhere I am guideless, untethered. I can't find half of me, or half of me does not want to leave, even though time could end that way. I cannot create in the way of my parents, who created me. Like most of the bees in the hive I have been privileged to observe, I am forever a daughter and sister, never a mother. Perhaps I did myself in a long time ago, stealing mourning dove eggs for show-and-tell and then abandoning them myself, or left my own power buried, lost in the piles of mysteries I've unraveled everywhere else.

[13] *In the Middle*

Out here, in the middle of the state of Wisconsin, in the middle of the continent, I can't seem to get to the center of things. Ponds and streams are guarded with grass; meadows and crop fields are vast and are only edged with paths. And the forests are hedges, so narrow that sky and prairie show clearly through the trees. Or, when I can't see through them, the forests are too brushy to enter, too full of species trying to regain a foothold that, in the ecological sense of the word, I'm not sure I can compete. I thought that moving to the heart of the country would make me long for edges, claustrophobic for the sea. But instead I find myself stuck on the periphery, unable to immerse.

I am a child of the woods. Meadows were things my sisters and I avoided as children; they were to be walked around, or, if necessary, gotten through quickly. Meadows were frightening: full of hairy stems and thorns, insect larva that left our thighs and knees covered in spittle. I grew up near corn, but farm fields out East were just stepping stones to forest, forests that seemed taller and deeper and darker than the forests here, forests that brought forth springs from the shallow soil under the roots of trees on the sides of hills, forests that held you without touching, that you could walk through with ease. In Maryland, you could always follow a brook to its beginning. The forests were all second-growth, I know, but they were a second older than here. And the second when they came of age also gave birth to me.

I am not of the mountains. But where I was born, in central Maryland, it was less than an hour's drive in three directions before the Appalachians would come into view.

"There they are!" my mother would exclaim, as soon as the shaggy brown line of lumps appeared along the horizon through the car window, just barely visible, like low clouds. She would turn from the front passenger seat to look at my sisters and me in the back of the car, as if to make sure we were straining to see the mountains as soon as we possibly could. They were like a distant relative, these mountains, someone we didn't see often, because we knew they were close, and that we could visit them if we wanted to.

I did not know that the simple things for which my parents created anticipation in my childhood would become exactly those things I would need in order to survive later on. I am not of the mountains, but I need them, like I need a family driving forward, and the shadow of a big woods that nearly encloses the place we'll return to soon.

About six months before we moved to Wisconsin, my husband and I decided to conceive a child. I saw many signs—an extra bright meteor that seemed to separate into several pieces, light rain after lovemaking, and once a parade of pullets—young turkeys—clucking softly and following their mother past our cabin just below our bedroom window.

But when I told a co-worker about the out-of-the-ordinary meteor he suggested it was just space junk—a piece of satellite or shuttle, a bolt, astronaut garbage—entering, and then burning up, in the atmosphere, hardly, I considered then, a symbol of new life.

In the high school where I teach now in Wisconsin, the science classes have made posters for the hallway. The posters hang vertically on long continuous sheets of paper down the high walls of the stairwell. Perhaps the students are learning how to scale things. One poster displays the position and thicknesses of the various layers of the earth from the core to the crust. On another—the one that draws my attention, actually stops me as I head to the car from my second floor classroom at the end of the day—the students have listed and spaced out the relative heights of several mountains. At the top lies Everest, at 29,035 feet, then Alaska's Denali, the tallest mountain in the United States, at 20,320 feet. Next is Mount Whitney in California, the tallest in the contiguous U. S., at 14,498 feet. Then they have listed the height of the North Rim of the Grand Canyon at 8,000 feet and, accordingly, the bottom of the canyon at 2,500 feet. I see something else, scribbled on the bottom edge of the poster, what at first simply looks like the result of a dropped, uncapped magic marker. No—the students have drawn in the third highest point in the state of Wisconsin, Rib Mountain, a popular, nearby ski hill. But at 1,924 feet—only 28 feet lower than Wisconsin's highest point—Rib Mountain doesn't even scrape the underbelly of the bed of the Colorado River. I avert my eyes and shake my head. I can't even hide from the terrain when I'm inside, for here it exerts itself on the poster like a sign, a banner, a flag for where I am now.

On the phone my mother tells me that my father has taken my Fisher-Price rock tumbler to the swap shop, along with a bundle of other things. "You should see how good our basement looks," she says. I'm disappointed, and we muse about the rock tumbler—a coveted former Christmas present of mine—turning in our cellar.

I remember filling the red plastic cylinder with water, a handful of rough agates that had come with the kit, and packets of progressively smaller sediments over the course of several weeks. The cylinder was set on a silver-gray base, all plastic, that was plugged in to turn for a few months. When you opened the cylinder, after the final weeks of churning with a fine white powder, the agates came out small and oval and patterned, ready to be glued to the cheap metal jewelry mounts that came with the kit.

But when I tried to tumble rocks I'd gathered on the grass-less banks that held our house up, it didn't work at all—or, really, worked too well. The rocks broke down too quickly, came out mud. Only a few gray ones that I had picked up on the railroad tracks survived, coming out round and slightly silver. But there weren't many of this kind—they were from somewhere else—and they were too large and too heavy to wear as jewelry.

Whenever I used it, no one in my family could block out the sound of that rock tumbler turning in the basement as we slept. The accordion door that separated the kitchen from the cellar steps was not enough to bar the constant whir of erosion happening below us. To everyone else it was mildly annoying, but me, I was curious, perhaps dangerously, of that sped-up un-building happening beneath the foundation of our home.

Other than Rib Mountain, the poster in the hallway at school does not display any peaks east of the Mississippi. And when I mention the Appalachians to my students, many of them crinkle their brows in confusion. Anyone who lives near the high, youthful Rockies, of course, hardly considers the ancient Appalachian range mountains. But the Appalachians still contain today some impressive heights, the highest being Mt. Mitchell in North Carolina, at 6,684 feet.

Once, on a backpacking trip, I trekked through the White Mountains of New Hampshire with a friend for a few days. I had planned a longer trip than she and after hiking out of the mountains and dropping her off where we'd parked one of our cars, I hiked back alone, heading toward the summit of Mt. Madison, at 5,366 feet. Everything was fine until I got above treeline.

Treeline is the point in a region at which trees stop growing due to unsuitable environmental conditions. Not all treelines occur on mountains. There can be desert treelines, indicating the most arid places trees can grow, arctic treelines, which refer to the farthest north trees can grow, and exposure treelines, referring to how near the windy coast trees can grow. On mountains, trees can be inhibited by all three of these factors: lack of water, cold temperatures, and too much wind.

The treeline in the Northern Appalachians is at about 3,500 feet. As you approach this point, because of, mostly, wind and poor soil, the trees that do survive get smaller and smaller until they are only as tall as you. Trees such as these, whose growth has been choked by wind, even have a special name: krummholz, which means crooked wood. They grow close, stunted and gnarled, with limbs all on one side or the other, flag-like. And then, suddenly, they are gone, and you step up and out of the forest as if it were a container, something that could hold you and let you go. All around you there is rubble. The trail is no longer walled by trees, but dotted by low cairns that topple and are rebuilt by good-willed hikers.

It wasn't that the cairns were absent or misleading; I knew exactly where to go. And this part of the trail was not particularly steep. It switch-backed up through the rubble for a couple more miles to a summit I couldn't yet see. It also wasn't the weather. The sky was clear and still. It may have been the lack of people—but I hadn't seen anyone for several miles all morning and it hadn't bothered me; perhaps the short-statured trees, like human twins, had been good company. For not long after I stepped above treeline, I was on my hands and knees on the rocks, my pack pulling me first to one side and then the other as I tried to steady myself, praying that I would not disappear. I walked from cairn to cairn bent and crying, looking back at the stunted trees, which skirted the mountain in a defined line as if a clan decision had been made that, for whatever reason, it just wasn't right or normal to go any higher.

Mountains for me have always failingly been connected with the potential for marriage and a family. I've bagged peaks with or because of my own short list of men: Old

Rag in Virginia with my high school English teacher, twenty years my senior; Mt. Pemmigewasset in New Hampshire with a lion-haired boy who was living out not quite the same camp counselor dream as I; the side of some unnamed hill in West Virginia with a PhD who shattered my wish to find a fossil by saying, after I confessed my wish, "They're everywhere," and picked up a rock that opened when he threw it at another to reveal some ancient fern or fish; and finally, Slide Mountain in the Catskills with a lawyer from New York who never showed up, leaving me the night before the climb, sleepless in a sort of mini-base camp at the foot of the mountain, listening to my tent's rain-fly flap in the wind and hearing the gruff, imagined voices of men saying, "She in there alone?"

Timm's Hill, the tallest point in Wisconsin, at 1,952 feet, is still not as tall as the bottom of the Grand Canyon. I used to joke with my husband when we visited the state before we moved here, when he would point out hills to me, that the hills were really just closed landfills that had been covered with sod.

And in fact, Timm's Hill is not part of an orogeny—some kind of ancient tension and uplift—though such events did occur billions of years ago in this region. Timm's Hill is the result of a recent cleaning that swept over most of the state. It is part of the terminal moraine of the Chippewa sublobe of the last glacier. Timm's Hill is a dump. It's basically a pile of rubble dragged and heaped together by the recession of the last ice sheet; it's an afterthought of a mountain, as if the glacier felt bad for leveling most of the rest of the state.

During my first year here, I carefully unfolded the map

and sought out all the high points: shorn volcanoes and outliers. They dotted the plains like sore thumbs; I had to reach them by successions of right-angled turns on roads that bordered farms, watching the high points rise singly in the distance a few hundred feet above the soy-fields, more like monuments than enclosing arms. I hiked the short paths to their summits. You just couldn't sneak up on them. And, in turn, they left me feeling exposed.

It's not really Wisconsin's lack of high elevations that has me feeling out of place. In fact, the house in which I grew up in Maryland is situated on a ridge at just 780 feet above sea level, two hundred feet lower than the house in which I live now in Wisconsin. True, the highest point in Maryland—Backbone Mountain, at 3,360 feet—is higher than Timm's Hill, but that is still a somewhat modest height, even for the Appalachians. What I'm really lacking in Wisconsin isn't mountains, but differentiation, the inability to wonder what is over the next rise, a reason to stay put, something to get lost in.

The geographic region in which I grew up was called the piedmont, defined by my dictionary as "a district or region lying along or near the foot of a mountain." Now I live in the central plain, defined as "an area of land not significantly higher than adjacent areas and with relatively minor differences in elevation, commonly less than 500 feet within the area." I once dwelled deep in a landscape characterized by its border, a rise in elevation; now I dwell in the opposite: land that seems to go on, indiscriminately, forever.

The only peaks I see out here are those I've brought with me, tucked away in a drawer in the nightstand beside the bed, on charts that show my temperatures rising that necessary six-tenths of a degree required for ovulation but never any higher, and always, in two weeks, dropping back down again. I think the months of patterns look normal, but, my doctor explains, there are many things that have to be just right in order for fertilization to occur, and something must not be right with me. My own growth stifled by unsuitable conditions, I feel dwarfed into being who I am now forever.

The place where I lay that night without the lawyer in the Catskills, hardly sleeping before the next day's icy April climb to just above treeline, was embraced by hemlocks on all sides. But it was likely completely barren of trees just two hundred years ago. Brought up on clocks whose every second ticked away a tree in the Amazon Rainforest, or one in our own Pacific Northwest, I have always been surprised by photographs of virtually anywhere in the Northeast from the 1800's. Such photos always show a simple cabin in front of a shockingly barren horizon. This is because deforestation was well under way in this area by the time the 18th century was rolling into the 19th. In 1839, New York was the leader in lumber production, providing 33% of the nation's timber. Maine, Pennsylvania, and New England combined provided another 30%. But by 1865, because the eastern U.S. had been virtually denuded, the timber industry moved west, making Michigan the leading producer. And by 1890, that leader was Minnesota. That means that somewhere in between 1865 and 1890 Wisconsin was stripped of its old-growth forest; the great north woods was peeled back from its level home and floated down river.

Some reports maintain that there is actually more forest

in the United States now than there was 300 years ago, forgetting to mention that many of these new forests are monocultures planted for lumber harvest. But the forests out east, the ones which held my sisters and me, the ones that grew on the ridge upon which our house stood and into the valleys on either side, and lined the rivers in both of those valleys, were unmanaged, mixed deciduous forests, and had already begun to regrow by the time the last huge pine was brought down in the great north woods of Wisconsin.

There was a chair on the side of the road where I walk my dog in the dark mornings, dropped as if it could go no farther, as if it had to take something sitting down, and even that was not enough. It lay on its back in the grass, looking up, its single central leg and whirl of three wheeled feet poised in midair. It startled my dog and me until the early sun revealed what it was, this solitary lump on the horizon. The next day it was gone.

And on our evening walk: a sandhill crane whose wet feathers on its thick, curled neck looked like matted fur. It poked up from the grass at the T-intersection I must go through to get to all points west. We approached it and it moved away, large and clumsy, but did not fly. I saw it from my car window at different points in the intersection all week; at first it seemed sick, then, as if it had something to decide.

But I can't make any meaning out of this: these metaphors that I didn't anticipate, which tease me on a flat road I can see and be seen on for miles, that never curves, that encloses nothing. For metaphors I must look to the mountains and the woods; I am krummholz, growing crooked and stunted, at the edge of where I belong.

I can understand how things can be not quite right for something: the land I stand on now, like the rocks I put in a childhood toy, is unreadable to me, erased to nearly nothing. For I am not of the mountains. But now I am nowhere, at a height above sea level that I cannot gauge because I cannot see it relative to anything. I am trying to enter this world, trying to stay in it, looking for trees that are at least more than seventy years old, and for my own son or daughter. These are my requirements for living—not for being whole, but for being part of something, for being in the middle.

[14] The Goddess of Wind Gets Married

There is something about the way a downed branch lies that tells you how long it has been on the ground. Of course, at this point on this particular trail—one that I walk often—rest other clues: many branches have been blown down, not just a few; none are covered with snow; and a couple show split wood as white as the meat from a chicken breast. But it's more than that. You can walk into any woods, even one where you've never been before, and recognize something that is newly fallen, recently wind-thrown. Among all the debris that combines on the forest floor, a newly fallen limb stands out like a piece from a different puzzle. It's from somewhere else, and instead of settling immediately, it hovers above the ground. It is still whole, has not yet begun to entwine with its new environment: the soil. Such limbs still reach for where they were, and look as if they are not done falling.

The storm windows rattled as the front blew in. The room shook its head, and lobed in sound, I dreamed. A blonde-haired woman in a field walked away from me. I caught up, took her by the shoulders, turned her around, and asked for a prophecy. But instead of telling my future, she told me what I was feeling. I reminded her of what she was supposed to do, recognizing, even in my state of sleep, this opportunity, but she only said, "Think about it." This is nothing like the prophecies I got in dreams ten years ago: second comings, components of the afterlife, the task of carrying my soul in a container of water.

Later, I dream that my lips have fallen asleep, like an arm or a leg might. They are completely numb, soaked with saliva, and, trying to wake them up, I begin to chew the insides of my cheeks, which does not hurt. It doesn't work, and my mouth swells with something like the filling from a cherry pie. I am forced to scoop out the contents with a finger and deposit them on the floor beside my bed, like one might do with the vomit of an unconscious person before efforts to resuscitate. I scream for my husband to help. He does not awaken, so I go to the bathroom to look in the mirror at my sleeping lips.

But when I get there, my lips diminish in importance to what they frame: a tooth, which loosens the more I look at it. According to where it is, it should be an incisor. It looks, however, like a canine, only it is a perfect equilateral triangle, and doubly serrated.

I do not associate wind with Maryland, the state where I grew up. On occasion it would moan through the rumpled metal roof of the dilapidated barn in the woods next to our house. But I never successfully flew a kite there, and wind did not balloon my shirts or catch my voice when I spoke before it got anywhere.

However, I do remember a friend, who, whenever we would drive, would roll the window of her blue Honda Accord all the way down and send a ferocious gale right into the car. She must, I thought, desire wind. Once, when she pulled suddenly but skillfully off the highway to park near a trailhead, she commented, pleased with herself and her car, "From 60 to 0 in a second." The words were from a commercial, but she said it as if it were her one line of dialogue in some grand epic. I decided she was acclimated to certain things—change, cold, wind—because she had just moved to Maryland from Green Bay, Wisconsin, and before that St. Paul, Minnesota, in between which—oddly enough, and unimaginably at that time—I would eventually end up living. This is where my future husband would be from, where the wind would rattle the storm windows while we slept in an old farmhouse.

My friend was exotic from all her travels. She had lived in Brazil from the age of three to six. She moved to my town as a sophomore in high school. When a spiteful history teacher put the impossible question of naming all of the republics of the former U.S.S.R. as extra credit on an unrelated test, she got every one. Her brother, she explained, had begun his education at a Montessori school, where he spent all his time tracing maps. It was his favorite thing to do. Somehow, it had filtered into her. Like wind, my friend was born on the move. I always admired the wind in her. It made her long blonde hair stream out, which somehow never got as knotty as mine.

In contrast, once, in third grade, my teacher unrolled the map of the United States that hung over the chalkboard and asked for a volunteer to come to the front of the room and point out Maryland. I knew I couldn't do it, but I raised my hand anyway, because everyone else had, and, of course— usually a sure bet for a correct answer—I was called on. I can still see the map at close range, a target I did not understand. I can feel my mind racing, unable to discern what element I should pull from memory—a color? a shape?—in order to point out my home state, where I had lived for, so far, all eight years of my life. My finger circled, hoping to zero in on something, pretending I knew where Maryland was but had lost it on my journey to the front. The class laughed good-naturedly behind me. I was mortified, unable to recognize something it was obvious I should know: a place, my home, in relation to the larger world. Could this be the first time I had seen a map? Unlike my future friend, who personified travel: Goddess of Wind, Adventure, Risk, I was utterly grounded. I completely lacked the skills to differentiate one place—even my home—from another.

There would be tension between us—between what we represented, her desire for adventure and my need for stability, tradition, a firm foundation—and also within us. And then there would be bewilderment, for what do you do when one of these—adventure, stability, either one—fails to produce what it's been promising all along?

Wind is caused by a difference in air pressure. It is really quite simple. Because earth is tilted on its axis—and because it is not uniform in color—it absorbs the sun's heat unevenly. Pockets of warm air rise above the land, creating areas of low pressure beneath them. Pockets of cool air sink, creating areas of high pressure. Wind occurs as air moves in a straight line from the area of high pressure toward the center of low pressure. The earth's rotation causes wind to turn, toward the right in the Northern Hemisphere, and toward the left in the Southern. And friction also affects it—if the wind is moving over water or smooth land it maintains its speed; forests or rough terrain will slow it down.

One thing the Goddess of Wind used to say about me was that I had a "place," and she was right. This place referred to a specific walk I took almost daily, through a cornfield near the home where I grew up, along a woods road, and down some ATV trails to a set of railroad tracks, and the creek that wound beneath them. My parents had taken my sisters and me and our leashed dog—whom we normally let run loose—there for a hike once when I was very young. After that one walk, during which the dog—a collie—would not cross the railroad bridges and sat down instead in the middle of the stream, refusing to ford, I somehow imagined that we had gone on this walk together every year, and would repeat it annually, like a holiday. The walk must have occurred at just the right, receptive period in my life, for I think it was then that I imprinted this particular activity— walking—and this particular habitat—the winding creek in the wooded valley—into my cache of behavioral responses and preferences. I don't think my parents and the dog ever went on this walk again, but my sisters and I did, and when they grew older I went alone, to see the train; to study, under the railroad bridge, for an English test; to get out of the house before I had a license; and then, even after I did have a license, to look for the things in the woods that by that time, after so much walking and seeing them year after year, had become my friends—bloodroot and butterfly weed, red-backed salamanders.

While I was walking through the woods and along the railroad tracks, commuting to a local college, still living with my parents, my friend went to school in Minnesota, dropped out, then moved to Hawaii with her boyfriend. After they broke up and he came back to the States, she spent a few months of vagrancy on the island, at times sleeping on the beach under a tarp with a stray dog she had claimed as her own. She sent me a postcard from Mt. Waialeale, the wettest place in the U.S. It looked high and lush. Then she came home, and while she planned an ice-climbing trip to Patagonia, interestingly, she found a stream near her own parents' house to hike along—Morgan Run—and she took me there once.

On one of these hikes, in the heat, we stopped at a place where the ten foot wide creek was squeezed to a human body's width between two large rocks, which deepened and smoothed its current. We had brought along a camera. While I would have been content to just sit next to the rapid and listen to it and watch it, she got the idea that each of us would take a picture of the other while she pressed her body into the flow of water and let it stream over her. Apparently, she had lain in such a way here before by herself. In the photo I took, my friend looks preserved in ice, eyes closed, the hint of a smile, an icon from some earlier world, not quite born, completely adaptable to this submerged environment, no oxygen. But I couldn't do it. I was afraid to make myself stay under. I just didn't fit. The water rushing over me threatened to move me, and I let it. In the picture she took, only a small percentage of my body is actually under the water. My face is pruned shut like a baby's. I'm all arms and legs, and the river is spitting me up.

I have a theory that it is windier here in Wisconsin than in Maryland, the land of my youth. At least once a week our newspaper ends up in the field across the street. In autumn, after the harvest, our yard becomes a carpet of cornhusks. During our first winter, our screen door wouldn't stay latched and we endured it repeatedly blowing open and banging arrestingly against the slate siding. Sometimes, even in summer, it is just so plain windy I don't even want to sit on the porch. But when I look for statistics, I can't find any proof. Mount Washington, out east in New Hampshire, is the windiest location in the United States. In fact, it holds the world record of the highest measured surface wind on earth—231 miles per hour on Thursday, April 12, 1934.

Wind can bring many things. Vayu, the Hindu God of Wind, blew off the top of a mountain, creating the island of Sri Lanka. Ehacatl, the Aztec God of Wind, brought physical love to the world. In Norse mythology, Njor is God of Wind, Sea, and Fire, and also brings good luck to hunters. His wife chose him by his feet, which were the cleanest of all the gods, although she thought she was choosing another. Amon, in ancient Egypt, was not only the God of Wind, but also the God of Fertility and secrets. Fei Lian, Chinese God of Wind, carries wind with him in a bag, and uses it to stir up trouble. Aeolus, from the Greeks, gave Odysseus a big bag of wind to help him find his way home which, unfortunately, his crew lost when they opened it.

I can't deny the influence the Goddess of Wind had on me. All those postcards from Hawaii, Colorado, her unvoiced disapproval of the first real job I took after college, which was in my hometown, provoked me to move out of my parent's house and into my first apartment. My own subsequent dislike of that job motivated a search for graduate schools out of state. True, one of my professors would ask me what I wanted to do after graduating, and I would list a few related jobs, then—more traditional than adventurous—confess what I really wished: to have children and raise them. Still, I attribute to my windy friend my ability to open up a map and plan a trip, because if she was somewhere, there was a reason to go—to Nebraska, to Maine. This newfound trip-planning ability is how I arrived to be looking at the clouds over Mt. Washington from the top of a neighboring peak, one I had summitted alone my second summer in graduate school.

I slept that night on the opposite side of Mt. Madison than the one I had backpacked up. I shared a campsite with two boys. I had tried to set up a makeshift shelter where the mountain was too steep for the full footprint of my tent, but a rumble of thunder sent me back to the head of the trail to take the two boys up on their initial offer to share their space. With one of the boys, I stayed up well into the night talking.

They had just come down from Mt. Washington. With the same kind of allure that the Goddess of Wind used when she spoke of some adventure, they encouraged me to leave my backpack at the campsite and hike to the top of Mt. Washington the next morning. But I suddenly felt I had been away from home too long. Heeding all the warnings about its quick and unpredictable changes in weather, not wanting to walk into the almost ever-present shroud that made Mt. Washington look like it was smoldering, for fear I would not come out, I pretended to sleep in while the boys packed up outside my tent. Then, in half an hour, without their knowing, I followed them out of the mountains and back to school, where in a few days I would meet the newest student, my neighbor, a boy with blonde hair from Wisconsin, as he was taking his bike off the back of his car. In two years we would be married.

A few weeks after my White Mountains hike, the late-night mountain boy sent me a book in the mail, with a letter written on the inside cover, which I read over and over. The book, which I still have not read, but my husband has, was Nicholson Baker's The Fermata, about a man who, as the jacket says, "likes to stop time and take women's clothes off."

Dreams about being scantily clad, of falling, of flying, and of losing a tooth are common, according to Freud's Interpretation of Dreams, something I perused in my teen years, when my dreams felt frequent and insightful: a belly covered in the eggs of wood frogs, a Jesus doll made of wax that turned its head to tell me something. Unsolicited, my mother sends me an email titled "Symbolism," and asks, referring to my recent dream, although she is a brunette, "Could I be the blonde-haired woman who couldn't tell you anything you didn't already know?"

Unsure, I turn to Freud and find, not surprisingly, that according to him parts of the face in dreams correlate to the genital area: the buttocks are represented by the cheeks, and—well, you can figure out the rest. If someone pulls out your tooth you are dreaming about castration. But in women, says a footnote that references Carl Jung, the losing of a tooth symbolizes birth. I think about the woman in the field now and what she had to tell me, let it surface, what I didn't think was important: that I should feel sad because I do not have a child. My numbed mouth, its fullness, the cherry-pie filling, the woman's message, and how closely it all fits the Jungian archetype is surprising. But it isn't helpful. Like the woman, the dream—even deciphered—doesn't tell me anything I don't already know. The wind brought the dream, and the dream brought me nothing, for the tooth wasn't quite right, and although it got looser and looser, it stayed put; it didn't fall out.

Average annual wind speeds on Mount Washington, although not nearly as high as the record, are still an impressive 45.3 miles per hour. Looking for support for my theory, I search for the country's windiest city, half expecting it to be in Wisconsin. But it is Dodge City, Kansas, which boasts an average annual wind speed of 13.9 miles per hour. Next ranks Amarillo, Texas, at 13.5 miles per hour, and then Rochester, Minnesota at 13.1 miles per hour. Two of those cities hail from the Midwest, I reason, and Minnesota is even North Central, like Wisconsin. But in Green Bay, Wisconsin, the average annual wind speed tops out at only 9.9 miles per hour. And Baltimore, Maryland, regardless of what I remember, is a bewildering 9.2, about the same.

In Wisconsin, I live on a 2.44 acre plot of land surrounded by wind breaks, supporting the fact that at least some person other than me believed this place was windy and that he or she needed to do something about it. In the front loom several very large, probably one hundred-year-old white pines which, despite nearly touching the house, are unable to keep the storm windows from rattling on those aforementioned windy nights. Rows of nearly as old silver maples line each side of the yard, their broad crowns countered by narrowly lobed leaves and deep sinuses. This makes them only somewhat effective at filtering the breezes that blow our hair flat across our faces during a game of horseshoes. At the back of the yard stands the most recently planted break, attesting the greatest support for my theory of the windiness of this place: a row of Chinese elms, a non-native, shrubby tree known for being planted especially in areas of high winds.

The first time the winds rattled the storm windows, my husband and I awoke and could not sleep. It was just after we'd bought the house, and we wondered if it was going to be a nightly thing. We finally rose and tried to brace the windows in their frames with socks and towels. This last time I awoke mid-rattle, deep in the night, and thought that I must be getting used to the sound. But then I lay awake for hours, until the dreams came. My husband and I no longer attempt to fill the spaces; we just wait for the storm to pass.

Often, when I watch the weather in winter in Wisconsin, the map will show that a cold, arctic air mass is moving down over the state. I find this exciting, even though it includes a bite of air that I have not yet taken, a new place to envelope me. I like the idea that air can exist over one piece of land, a province in Canada for example, and then move down over another piece of land quite distant from its origins. I like the idea that the air stays together in one big mass, and that when it moves, it leaves the land beneath it stable, but wherever it goes, it changes things altogether abruptly for a few days, even a week or so.

In winter, the weather pattern I am used to anticipating is the Nor'easter. Of course, I remember the Nor'easter mostly for the snow it brought that kept us home from school; drifts—and the wind that created them—were a novelty. But the Nor'Easter, I am surprised to find, is a storm defined by its winds, described as an area of low pressure just off the Atlantic coast that sends gale force winds, and often inches of snow or rain, to states from Maine to Virginia.

Gale force winds, according to the Beaufort scale, which ranks wind on a continuum of 1-12, are listed as a 7. Gales set whole trees in motion, and effort is needed to walk against such winds. According to the scale, at 2, where wind is called a light breeze, leaves begin to rustle. At 4, designated a moderate breeze, dust and loose paper are raised. At 6, a whistling can be heard in overhead wires, and, the scale quaintly cautions, umbrellas become difficult to use. I wonder where Beaufort was standing when he made this scale, jumping effortlessly from place to place—the woods, outside an office building, at a power-plant, in the rain.

I search for the name of a Midwestern wind, ready to acknowledge what I am experiencing. I look through lists of names. Some are quite specific—the Fremantle Doctor, for instance, which is described pleasantly as "an afternoon sea breeze from the Indian Ocean which cools Perth, Western Australia during summer." But I find nothing for Wisconsin. Here, winds are named simply for the direction from which they come.

Last Christmas, as my husband and I made the long drive from Wisconsin to Maryland, our car wavered in its lane. I was quietly satisfied, cutting Southeast at 75 miles per hour towards Interstate 80 against this force that seemed to want to make me stay, this force that beckoned, but also trapped. It was difficult to rate the car's competition because we were already in motion—through the window I was hard pressed to find small trees swaying. This would make the wind a Beaufort 5, moving from 8 to 10.7 miles per hour, enough, perhaps, to affect our driving. When we stopped for gas, though, we saw that we'd left the hood slightly open; we'd checked the oil before leaving. The air felt relatively calm, and the rest of the ride was much smoother.

Once we reached Maryland, I met the Goddess of Wind in a local bar over the holiday. We hoped to see anyone from our graduating class—an informal, unplanned reunion. She had come from Lawrence, Kansas, where she had been living for five years after moving there to obtain her art degree and a position teaching in a Montessori school. It was where she and her fiancé would be residing: the middle of the country. Lawrence has, of the five Kansas cities for which I can later find statistics, a moderate annual average wind speed, like Baltimore and Green Bay, of just 9.9 miles per hour.

In the bar, the Goddess of Wind pulled out her digital camera to show me pictures of a wedding dress she was considering. We leaned over the displayed image, holding the camera between us like a GPS unit, in that smoky room where we no longer knew anyone. She zoomed in until the entire screen was white, using the arrow keys to travel down a path of beads along the back of the dress. It was not a landscape we had thought she would ever be navigating, and

I wondered what it would mean for me when the Goddess of Wind settled down. But I nodded my approval, and we giggled in disbelief at what she was finally doing.

At last, I find it. On a wind resource map of the United States, which rates the ability of the wind in each state to be used to generate power, I find that there is an accepted, measured difference in the wind between here and where I grew up. Central Maryland is rated as class 1, or poor, and Central Wisconsin is, just as I suspected, slightly windier at class 2—marginal. It doesn't bother me that according to this map I'm barely experiencing wind at all—it's the difference, not the amount, that I'm fixated on. I wanted documentation that this place is windier than where I grew up because it doesn't feel like home. And now I've got it—and more, evidence that the wind I'm experiencing is classified as unproductive.

Two or three nights before the wedding of my windy friend, before we had left for Kansas, I dreamed about her. She called to tell me she had been in a car accident. She was not upset. She had lost both her legs, but was still going through with the wedding. When I saw her, both legs had been amputated below the knee, but where there should have been rounded nubs, the bone and skin had been chiseled to very fine points, as if she were walking on two pencils.

When we arrived in Kansas I told her I had dreamed about her, thinking, lover of adventure, she would appreciate the weirdness, but something inside made me stop before explaining the dream any further. It was not the time or the place, I realized, for in two days she would be wearing that image from the camera, like a new continent, her hands full of flowers. She would request a mint from her maid of honor, a straightening of her veil, a touch-up on her lipstick from her future sisters-in-law, while we waited to process out for the ceremony. We would be wearing dresses the color of a very pale winter sky and, Dorothy-style, with all their magic, shiny red shoes.

Back in Wisconsin, the just-fallen branches I noticed so long ago no longer look new. Their needles have lost their rigidity, without life to counter gravity. Although some of them still point up, they look propped instead of moving. The once-white breaks in the woody tissue have become moist and have begun to brown. Soon, these branches will be indistinguishable from what has been five or six months down. They will no longer be fallen limbs; they will have become sticks and soil. But no matter how much time passes, I can't help but feel, I will still be visible. In spite of whom I used to be, I am not the goddess of staying put, of inertia, at least not here. Perhaps it is my unwillingness to stay, to even have come in the first place, my inability to procreate; I will stand out against this land. For I am an easterly wind, and as my feet skim the path at three miles per hour an average of twice a week on this little stretch of land, I cannot shake the sensation that I am only half-awake, dreaming fruitless dreams, and I have not yet hit the ground.

[15] Deranged

When I come to this part of the trail, my perspective is all wrong. I anticipate that the rise I have just walked up will reveal a linear valley on the other side; I expect to find a creek at the bottom, a sinuous path with two options for travel: upstream or down. For an instant, I am almost home.

But the rise descends to a bowl, a landform I can't register. It directs me nowhere but around its rim or to its center. I've reached a glacial kettle—a depression in the plains—the steep sides of which no one could farm, so they are covered with trees and the basin with sedges, submerged in water for a few months each year and now flattened with snow.

About 80% of the precipitation that falls on earth lands directly in the oceans. Of the 20% that falls onto land, some gets locked up in glaciers and snow fields, and some seeps directly into the soil as groundwater. Less than 1%, about 36,000 cubic kilometers per year, becomes runoff, and returns to the oceans by my favorite thing in the world: a crick.

At least, that is what my sisters and I called the one

that ran in the valley behind our house, until classmates—including a friend who lived just downstream from us—made fun. Although I've trained myself to use "creek" now instead of "crick," I still can't hear the vowel sound in crick as an altered long e, as if we had pushed the double e in the correct spelling of the word into too narrow a space. A crick is different from a creek. A crick is its own entity. You can never jump over it, yet you can barely swim in it. It is perfect for wading, but you have to watch out for crayfish, and broken glass, and things like a flap of burlap feed sack caught on a rock along with some long grasses. Once, the water had risen and flowed over such a jam, smoothing it into skin and hair, until my sister and I thought we were looking at a drowned child.

The dictionary indicates that crick is used for creek in the northern and western United States, areas to which my family and I had never been. For the crick we followed flowed solidly through the state of Maryland and into the Chesapeake Bay; it was the East Branch of the Patapsco River. I don't know how the word trickled into my parents' vocabulary. For a while my downstream friend and I solved the problem of what to call it by compromising, and it became the "criver," a combination of what I called it and what it had been officially dubbed. But somehow, this moniker never felt right; it made the situation feel polygamous, and when we played in the criver, in a way, I felt like I was cheating on the crick, on what it, and what I, really were.

I used to watch some small percentage of that 36,000 cubic kilometers—an odd shape in which to imagine water—form rills in our front yard during a storm. It must have been soon after our house was built, before anything—moss or weeds—took hold in that muddy, rock-strewn strip of yard under the trees; it must have been when I was very young and propped myself up on the couch to look out the picture window like my nieces do now. For I remember being caught in the current, mesmerized by a yard of streams and the possibility of playing in them. In spite of the rain, I couldn't make the connection. I had no idea where these full-fledged streams came from, and why it was when the storm was over and I could go outside, they suddenly disappeared, leaving snake-like scars in the mud as incomprehensible as the surface of Mars.

Only one other time did I witness this particular act of creation, playing at the house of the downstream friend, in her woods, which began halfway down the side of a steep cornfield, with the criver at the bottom. It was crisscrossed with deep, dry gullies to which we never gave a second thought until the day—we were old enough to play out in the rain now—we spent waist-high in channels of turbulent muddy water. It ran in sheets off the cut field and into gullies that funneled it down to the criver. At first, we made a game of fording, but eventually just stood in the filled corridors, gorging ourselves on the speed of the water.

When I was little, I lived in the Gunpowder-Patapsco watershed, which drained into the Chesapeake Bay, and then into the Atlantic Ocean. Now, in Wisconsin, I live in the Wolf River watershed, but I can hardly tell. Around here, I just can't get a feel for where things are going. I had to look it up.

My source defines individual watersheds, or drainage basins, as a river and all of the smaller tributaries that lead into it. Watersheds are separated by areas of higher terrain called divides. The Continental Divide, which runs along the Rocky Mountains of the United States, is an obvious one, dictating whether run-off will flow east or west across the continent. But some divides, the source says, such as that which separates the Great Lakes drainage basin from the Mississippi Drainage basin—precisely where I live now— are what it calls "rather modest rises."

This is why, when I am at the little kettle with its steep walls, I feel like I am almost home. The divides between watersheds I grew up in were quite high, high enough for names like "killer hill," steep enough for a neighbor's cow to tumble off and end its life. So when I find something more than a modest rise, I can't help but glance toward the bottom for moving water. I still believe it will be there, and when it is not, I am continuously surprised.

In Finksburg, Maryland, we were part of the watershed. We walked it every day, up the driveway and up the road from where the school bus dropped us off. In fact, at 731 Ridge Road, we lived atop one of those divides. Out the back door, about a half-mile's walk, was the East Branch of the Patapsco. Not until many years later—probably because it involved crossing a road—did we discover that out the front door about the same distance was the West Branch. Both branches were easy to get down to, but both entailed long, tiresome walks home. Soon, simply crossing them turned to following along the cricks in braided paths, first on one side, and then the other. We were like the northern water snake my oldest sister and I once saw with a fish three times its width in its mouth, washing downstream, unable to navigate but unable to give up what it had bitten into. We would follow the crick for hours, in old tennis shoes or bare feet, and then climb up into someone's back yard and circle home on the road.

And so like water, we had this choice of where to spend a summer afternoon; along the East Branch were rocky banks and an old woods road. Along the West Branch were the ghosts of railroad tracks, tie-less rails with their rock-beds long since swept out from under them, curving up, for one who could balance on them, to gap-tied bridges with crumbling trestles. And both rivers met at the swimming hole, behind the house where my mother grew up, what my father called the mud-seal, when he would come up from the city to visit his cousins and swim in it as a child. This was many years before he met my mother.

This pattern of cricks that lead predictably to one another has a name. It is called dendritic, one of several types of drainage recognized by hydrologists. The dendritic drainage pattern is the most common. From an overhead view it is arborescent, which means resembling a tree, with smaller tributaries conjoining successively larger streams and rivers. It is found especially on gently sloping terrain where the underlying rock erodes all at the same rate.

There are several other, less common types of drainage patterns, all of them easy to imagine. In a rectangular pattern—which looks like a cactus—streams bend and conjoin at relatively right angles. This regularity is caused by right-angle joints in the underlying bedrock, which erode more easily and create stream channels, such as on the Colorado Plateau. A trellis pattern, which looks to me like sutures on a wound, occurs where there is a series of parallel ridges and valleys, as in central Pennsylvania and northwest New Jersey. There, large streams flow parallel to one another in the lowlands, and are joined by smaller tributaries flowing at right angles down the mountains. Much more exotic sounding is the radial pattern. Radial defines water that flows down in all directions from a central point, such as might be found on a series of volcanoes. There are others, but none quite like the one that describes how water moves where I live now. I can't figure it out from the ground, and in a physical geography textbook the drawing looks like the Rorschach test, a smashed spider, an accident. The term that describes the drainage pattern in all but the southwestern corner of Wisconsin: deranged.

There is one other river that rivaled the East and West Branches of the Patapsco for my love: the Big Flatbrook, in Sussex County, New Jersey. Like the Patapsco, it was wade-able but barely deep enough in most parts for a dip. But it was mostly devoid of broken glass, had virgin hemlock forest on both banks, and was full of class one animals: mayflies and stoneflies, both indicators of very clean water. This, and the fact that I was older when I met it, kept me from dubbing it a crick. The Flatbrook River was also where I met my husband, where we hung a swing on a fat, arching yellow birch that held for five years and may still be holding. We would each go there one at a time, and leave a note for the other to come. Once, I found a crown of ferns on the wooden plank we used to cross where one bank got too dense to follow, so you can see why I left with him.

There are cricks in Wisconsin. My husband's uncle has one in his back yard in New Berlin, and I swear I heard someone in his family refer to it by jamming the long e's together to form that familiar word. But, with the exception of the driftless area, the area of Wisconsin that was not glaciated in the last period of glaciation, Wisconsin cricks do not surround you like the branches of a tree; they are not numerous. And because the terrain is relatively flat, you mostly cannot climb their banks. The drainage pattern here is not dendritic. In the section of the state where I live, it is termed deranged.

Deranged means the land was recently altered, disrupting previous drainage patterns, and the water has not yet organized itself into a system. In this type of drainage, streams flow in irregular directions in and out of lakes and swamps. My source uses Minnesota, Wisconsin, and Michigan as its prime examples of deranged drainage patterns. For they are where, 10,000 years ago, glaciers dumped sediments to create water-holding swamps, and dropped rubble onto streams, impounding them into lakes. The book maintains that the states' "previously established drainage systems were obliterated by the glacial ice." Obliterated. Where I walk now, water has not yet found its way—like I in this new land.

So, river-less, I hike along the terminal moraine of that aptly named Wisconsin glacier. I follow the print of this mile-thick ice-block, which, during the last ice age, molded a hilly, elongated, backward S across the face of the state at its farthest reaches, flattening the rest. I hike not along a creek, but in its memory.

Sometimes I walk on an esker, the bed-load of a river that flowed beneath the incredible weight of the glacier as the glacier began to melt. Think of it as an underground river with banks and roof of ice instead of rock, depositing sediment for a thousand years or so. When the river changed course or dried up, and the glacier dissipated, all that was deposited would be revealed as a tiny snaking rise amidst the surrounding landscape. I hike on this inverted river, not water, not mountain, simple dust, indicative of something that was, like the path of a comet.

Mostly I hike to a kettle, a depression left by a chunk of ice that broke off from the receding glacier. These chunks were covered in and surrounded by silt and sand and pebbles deposited as the glacier continually advanced and receded above them. Finally, the chunks themselves melted, resulting in large potholes in the land's surface. I sit on the rim of the pothole and my eyes walk its circular summit, trying to read what is there instead of trying to see what I remember.

I rejoice in the uphill these kettles provide, and continue to provide: the land rises about a half inch per year as a result of isostatic uplift, in which forces that tend to elevate balance those that tend to depress. The land can still feel the glacier's pressure. It is still responding. The result is that the land is 160 feet higher than it was when the last glacier rested where I now walk.

I rejoice in this uphill because just a few miles from here begins the Central Plain, what used to be the bed of Glacial Lake Wisconsin. A lobe of ice once dammed the Wisconsin River, spreading it over an area the size of Great Salt Lake. Now drained, that area is flat and sandy. I may be lost, but I am lucky: according to the locals, I live in the hills. Each time I walk a narrow path that cuts along the side of one ascent I pause at a cow-sized, pink lump of granite, a glacial erratic poised for ten thousand years in this very place, dragged from its home and then dumped here when the cold could hold it no longer. I'm grateful for this edge of up and down upon which I can venture, which creates through its varied terrain a real sense of motion and unknowing even without streams.

And I am learning that when I step off the road and into this kettle I will not be greeted by a crick. I will not be greeted with that familiar picture, imprinted on my brain from growing up in a dendritic watershed: a river at the bottom of two steep faces, which carries the watcher along with its ever-closer parallel lines between two overlapping hills and away. But I will be greeted just the same, with a sound: the creaking of a chair, a high, ascending trill, a rattling horn. For in the spring this kettle fills, and if I stay there will be colonies of friends, both old—wood frogs and spring peepers—and new—sandhill cranes.

[16] Kame

For nearly a year the kame hides, its peak and steeply sloping southern face concealed behind rows of planted pines; a mixed deciduous forest obscures its other three sides. But beneath the trees, the kame protrudes from the gently sloping cheek of the glacier's moraine like a pimple.

Wherever there is varied terrain, trees in the low points, competing for sunlight, will grow as tall as trees on the summits, so that, from above, one has to look very closely to discern the shape of the land beneath what it nourishes. So it is around the kame: what appears to be a modestly inclined ridge—one that extends as far east and west as the edge of the glacier did itself, and has been permitted to retain forest because it is slightly too steep to farm—masks a detailed topography. Since moving to the Midwest, I have been yearning for something to walk up, a pinnacle, a vantage point, and here in the woods behind my house, beyond the farm-field, has been hiding something which, to my worn-out eyes, has all the marks of a mountain.

I am fooled for weeks into thinking the two bands of

pine at the base of the kame actually represent two different species, they are so different in age. The lower swath, too young to bear the red mosaic of bark which distinguishes the older, higher swath as red pines behind it, I assume are white pines, until I look up from the deer-marked snow and notice the needles I brush with my entire un-streamlined body as I cut through them. The needles are the length of my palm, in pairs. It's unmistakable. These are red pines, too, and it's only a matter of years before they bear the ruddy skin of their elders.

It has been seven years since I married, three years since I moved to Wisconsin, four years since my husband and I decided to start a family. When I think about the smooth silvery sheen on the slim trunks of these young red pines, how it is nearly impossible to identify new trees by their bark, I wonder what a child of ours might be like. I consider the traits our child could inherit: he would likely sit with his thumbs crossed left over right, be able to roll his tongue, have earlobes adherent, no dimples, and only a small chance of blue eyes. He might be conscientious, artistic, and conventional. He may or may not be extraverted, agreeable, or religious. But whatever he was, he would be 50% me and I would be 50% him, my closest relation, after my own parents pass away, on the planet. He would begin with a cell from my own body, and continue living after I died, and although it is selfish, I will say it: he would keep me alive. Children, I think, are the reason we go on living when we know we will only die.

Soon the young red pines will wear the scaly, red outer covering of the aged stand behind them, where, too numerous for a property line or a hiking trail, shoulder-height blazes of paint, redder than bark, mark every other tree in several rows. For these are planted pines, and they will be taken for lumber, perhaps revealing what has been here all along, what I am headed for: the kame, a rise—distended and hard—in the land where I will spend my adulthood.

Jared Diamond cites the now barren Easter Island as not only the most extreme example of forest destruction in the Pacific, but one of the most extreme examples in the world. I lie down to read his essay, "Twilight at Easter," in the afternoon sun on my couch. The couch is a mission style piece with oak veneers. The dog is asleep in a similar square of sun on our maple floors in the next room. I descend easily through Diamond's logic.

Easter Island, settled by Polynesians around 900 AD, once supported a sub-tropical rainforest. In that rainforest was the world's largest palm tree, now extinct. Besides eating the tree's nuts, islanders would have used the sap for wine, the leaves for roofs, and the trunks for rafts. Other trees in this forest were used by the Polynesians to create ropes and ladders necessary for erecting the huge stone statues for which the island is famous, statues created to show status to rival clans.

But overuse of the forest's products, as well as the clearing of the forest for crops, likely set into motion a chain reaction that eventually led to the island's abandonment. Without trees for nesting, land birds and other wild food sources began to disappear. Without trees to make rafts and canoes, the islanders could no longer hunt their major food source—dolphin. This lack of available protein would lead eventually to cannibalism between the clans. The emptied forest would also require a switch to the toppling of statues, rather than their erection—an important distinction—to show status. By the time Europeans arrived in 1722, the island was devoid of human life.

After reading the article, however, I'm not sure I'm left with the intended effect. The sun has warmed the couch cushions almost to my body temperature, and although I get it—Diamond's warning about "self-inflicted environmental damage," the potential humans have to pollute themselves off of the planet—I feel strangely content, satisfied by how things can make so much sense. It's as if there was no problem to solve, as if simple awareness, for me at least, were an end in itself. For it's difficult—and this, I believe, is both my saving grace and our tragic flaw—to feel sad for a desolate future too deeply and too long, when one is alive in the present.

The geologic feature that I have been so delighted to find near my new home is called a kame, a word from a Northern Scottish dialect that signifies a small, steep-sided hill. You will find kames in Scotland, and here in Wisconsin, as well as in other places where glaciers have changed the landscape.

I can only reach the kame during about six months of the year. The walk involves crossing a half mile of field which last summer was planted with soy, and the summer before with corn. When the growing season is over, and the muddy ground is frozen, the kame is accessible. But occasionally, both before and after the growing season, the farmer comes with his spreader and covers the field, inch by inch, with a deep, brown, wet blanket of liquefied cow manure and—I find from the man who comes to pump out our septic tank— human feces as well. With that in mind, when I walk, I let my dog relieve herself on the field, and I don't clean it up.

Kames are conical shaped piles of sediment up to one hundred feet high. Some accounts describe their formation as the result of a hole in a glacier, and although it probably didn't happen that smoothly, that is the simplest way to imagine it. Sediment carried by a stream on top of a glacier would travel down this hole, piling its bed-load there and, when the glacier receded, it would leave behind a steep mound, like sand that has lost its hourglass casing.

The first time I hike up the kame, I realize I've found something precious: this hill is like none I've ever climbed. About halfway up there is a sort of tree-line. I've hiked past many tree-lines: at 3,500 feet above sea level in the Appalachians, and 7,000 feet above sea level in the Rockies, the climate becomes too cold and the soil too sparse for trees to survive.

The top of this hill is 1190 feet above sea level. The point from which I walk to it—my house—sits at 1000 feet above sea level. But the first 100 feet of rise are spread out over almost a mile, a gentle slope covered in crops for most of the year, barring the farthest segment, which holds the planted pines. The last 90 feet of rise—the actual kame—occur over just 450 feet of distance. The kame is steep and, relative to its surroundings, high. Standing at its base before hiking up it and looking toward one's destination is comparable to looking up at a high-rise, a building of at least twelve floors, or 115 feet in height.

Although 1190 feet is too low for a tree-line, after a relatively consistent point up the kame's base, there are no trees. But the older band of red pines planted at the bottom is almost as tall as the kame's summit, and trees on the hillock behind and on both sides are taller. From the window where I write this now, you would never know that there is a near-perfect polygon with a clear vantage of your life hiding in the woods behind you. From the bottom of the kame, and as I hike up it the first couple times, because of its symmetry, it seems almost unnatural, like an Egyptian pyramid, or the ones I visited in Mexico on my honeymoon.

It has been suggested that the word honeymoon comes from the Norse word "hjunottsmanathr," which refers to the ancient practice of a man abducting his woman of choice from a neighboring village and keeping her in hiding until one of two things happened: either she got pregnant, or her family and friends stopped looking for her. For the more sentimental, honeymooning has been related to the Northern European custom of having the bride and groom drink a cup of honeyed wine each day for the first month of their marriage. Despite the folklore, the term "honeymoon" most probably dates back to only the sixteenth century, and simply describes that brief, waning period of early marriage when life is sweet and good.

I met my husband in a New Jersey state forest. The day after I met him, on my suggestion, we hiked in the Appalachians. We ate lunch at a pond surrounded by hemlocks. That fall we hiked to the top of Slide Mountain, the tallest mountain in the Catskills, and I taught him how to use a compass. A year and a half later, atop Jupiter's boulder in Black Rock Forest in the Hudson Highlands of New York, we decided to get married.

Then came plans for the hjunottsmanathr. I suggested

an eco-tour in the Galapagos Islands, or backpacking in the Canadian Rockies. I argued to go to many different places; Cancun was not one of them. But once we arrived in Mexico, I did want to visit the ancient Mayan city of Chichen Itza.

After a brief guided tour, we were left on our own to explore the vast Mayan ruins, and like most we gravitated toward the Pyramid of Kukulkan. This pyramid, which served the Mayans as both a calendar and a place of rituals, is the tallest ruin at the site. With a base of 60 square yards and a height of 117 feet, it towers above the surrounding jungle, precipitous, like my kame over the farm-fields.

I can't help but think about that pyramid as I switchback up the kame, trying to lesson the effort required to get to the summit. Each face of the Pyramid of Kukulkan features 91 steep steps with narrow treads, which lead to a small, square temple at the top. At the time we visited, only two of the pyramid's four sides had been restored to become climbable; one of them included a single chain down its center for the climbers to cling to. This side, however, was teeming with tourists, so my husband and I opted to climb and descend the pyramid unaided.

Making it up was easy. We flew past the out-of-shape, old and young alike huffing and puffing in the heat and I thought, for a Wisconsinite—a flatlander—my husband set an excellent pace and had good hiking thighs. But after the three or so minutes of ascending, when I turned to look down from the temple at the top, I suddenly found myself barely able to breathe. I backed flat against a crumbling limestone wall, afraid to move, but the expansion and contraction of my lungs threatened to throw me off balance. I took only shallow breaths, unable to stop imagining myself tumbling over the side.

I watched my husband maneuver and skip through the crowd to get all the best views. I was not about to attempt this slalom around faceless men, heads hidden behind video cameras, any of whom might push me off the narrow edge by accident while reaching for a cigarette. I felt like a toothpick balanced on the head of a pin, as if the slightest breeze could send me end over end down the near-vertical slide which masqueraded as thin steps, all the way to the ground. After about thirty seconds of this, I was seated, terrified, inching my way back to level ground, step by step, on my rump.

In my research of the word kame, I come across a myth that is unrelated, but which I cannot forget, for it virtually attributes creation to a mountain. It is about Kamè, who, according to the Kaingang—a group of Amerindians from Southern Brazil—is one of the twin creator brothers. According to the myth, at one time, all of the land inhabited by the ancestors of the Kaingang, except for one mountain— like my kame, I imagine—was submerged in water. Kamè and his brother Kairu swam toward the mountain, with sticks of burning firewood in their mouths. The two drowned, and their souls went to live in the mountain's center, but as recorded by Telemaco Borba, the first to publish the Kaingang origin myth in 1882, "after much labor, they came out by two paths." It is as if the mountain gave birth.

Kamè and Kairu then proceeded to create the beings of nature. Kamè worked during the day, Kairu worked at night. Kamè made the pine, Kairu made the cedar. Kamè, the lizard, Kairu, the monkey. When Kamè made the jaguar, Kairu began making an animal to combat it. But when the sun began to appear, he had still not made the teeth, tongue, and some of the toenails. Since he could not work during the day, he quickly put a stick in the animal's mouth and told the animal that since it had no teeth, it would live eating ants. That is why, according to the Kaingang, the anteater is an imperfect and unfinished animal, as were most of Kairu's creations, while Kamè's were in general perfect and dangerous.

The kame differs from other high points I've experienced because although no trees grow beyond a certain point on its front face, the kame itself is nested in forest. And while from the bottom the kame looks unnaturally angular, oddly enough, from the top it looks unnaturally rounded, so that when I sit at its summit on a patch of matted grass where the snow has melted away, I feel I am sitting atop an egg.

I watch my dog, who has beat me to the top, bolt back toward the descent. The sides are so steep and, from my viewpoint, so seemingly rounded, I am almost frightened; I think that she will tumble to the bottom, as I feared I would in Chichen Itza, and probably break a leg. But she comes to a complete stop and pauses there on the convex side, appearing as I imagine humans must look standing on the earth from outer space. And it is as if the kame is large enough for its own gravity to have pulled it into a globe-like shape.

On my own descent, I stop to look at the soil's surface beneath the matted grass where the snow has melted. Between the tufts is an array of differently colored and differently shaped rocks. Some are smooth and almost pebble-like. Others are more angular. They range in size from silt to rubble-stones that fit in my palm. This makes sense. Kames are composed of what a river once carried and then dumped, if not underneath the glacier, then along its edge. Such sediment is called "unsorted" or "unstratifed." Although the ground is frozen, I manage to pull up five or six different rocks, and I carry them home in my pockets. I wonder how long it would take me to dismantle the entire thing, a few pretty rocks at a time. I sit the rocks on the kitchen table, and later in the week they get moved to the top of the microwave. I imagine the entire kame transported, laid out on all the surfaces in the house—the seats of the chairs, the bed, the bathtub—sorted and arranged into like piles.

The Mayans, according to Jared Diamond, are another culture that collapsed due to self-inflicted environmental degradation. There were 50 million members of this native Mexican tribe by 800 A.D. They had the most advanced writing in the new world, and were extremely gifted at astronomy. They built huge cities complete with ceremonial platforms, palaces for the elite priestly class, pyramids, temples, observatories, and ball courts.

But, like the Polynesians on Easter Island, they cut down all their trees. Excavations of building foundations in the Maya-inhabited Copan valley in Western Honduras, for example, show that buildings in the bottomlands became covered in sediment sometime during the eighth century. The Mayans had a serious problem with erosion. The hillsides had been deforested for fuel and for materials to make plaster for architecture, as well as to open land for settlement by an increasing population. The acidic soils which eroded from these hills probably decreased agricultural yields in the farmed bottomlands by changing the chemistry of the soil.

Furthermore, due to the role trees play in water cycling, mass deforestation can be a factor in causing drought. And drought, a major threat to farming, is commonly believed to be a cause in the collapse of Mayan civilization. Few signs have been found indicating anyone in the Copan Valley after 1235. By the time Cortez arrived in the 16th century, it is estimated that up to 90% of the peak Mayan population of 50 million had died out or dispersed, most in the previous one hundred years.

I could gather rocks all the way down to the base of the kame. They must tumble to the bottom when it rains but instead of siding up against some ancient abode, they simply rest in the sandy soil between the bands of young and old pines. As I walk toward home, behind me, the older red pines tower over my head; in front of me, I can almost see over the younger ones to the unplanted field which would probably also be covered in the kame's progeny, the rocks it sheds, were it not for the pines' roots.

Briefly, standing in the gap between young and old pines, I stare at the two stands, trying to age them. Did the Polynesians know they were extirpating the world's largest palm tree 1,100 years ago? I feel foolish for previously misidentifying the younger pines, although, according to writer Donald Culross Peattie, in early America, red pine was often simply conceded to be white pine where the two were harvested and sold together.

Now that I know what they are, I have searched for what else there is to know about them. It can take a red pine seedling 4-10 years to reach a height of just 4.5 inches, barely the rim of my boot, so even the young ones here must be many years older than me. Red pines don't even begin to bear seeds until 15-25 years of age; in closed stands like these it is usually much later, not until age 50 or 60. And their children are unique—in the world of trees, that is. Red pines are one of the most morphologically homogeneous pines that exist. This means that there is not much genetic variability between individual red pine trees.

It is believed that, during the last ice age, or possibly much earlier, red pines experienced a population bottleneck. In other words, they were reduced by some outward factor, such as the glacier, to a small, isolated population, which limited their diversity. These small, isolated populations limited their diversity by increasing their propensity to self-propagate, resulting in children genetically identical to their parents, versus reproducing sexually, which would result in children with variable genetics. In the world of red pines, your child is likely to be your twin, a clone, an exact replica, 100% related, at least genetically.

But this puts red pines in a delicate position—without variability, a disease could conceivably wipe out the entire species. Nearly one-third of the acres of forest in Northern Wisconsin are red pine plantations, which makes for a frighteningly easy target. It has also been predicted that, because of warmer summers—potentially due to human-caused global climate change—the red pine will be extirpated from the United States before the end of the 21st century.

Did the Polynesians on Easter Island, or the Mayans, make predictions about trees, about soil? Perhaps their losses were necessary for us to evolve the ability, or the motivation, to predict at all. And what comes after predictions anyway—what word? Can we name it—what we should do, this collective, precautionary action that will save us all? Can we carry it out, or has it been more adaptive, so far, just to ignore it?

At the top of the pyramid of Kukulkan, during my honeymoon trip to the abandoned city of Chichen Itza, I sought solace in the little temple for a few minutes of shade in a meager attempt to regain my sense of balance. To my surprise, a small brown dog wearing no collar was lying in a shallow ditch hollowed by water in a corner of the room. It was a hot day; he was panting, and as all dogs do when they pant, tongue lolling out, he appeared to smile. For a few seconds I forgot about my own discomfort; I worried, wondered, and marveled about the little dog, about how he had gotten up and how he would be getting down. But it only lasted half a minute, for at all costs, at the time, I needed to get myself off the top of the pyramid and safely down to level ground.

Now I spend full half hours at the top of my kame, on its barren summit, while my dog runs up and down, up and down, a dozen times before my eyes. I love it here, and so does she. From the tops of some of the pyramids of the Mayans, it is said, you can see the tops of the pyramids of other rival Mayan cities. When I stand I can see the house in which I write, and the road at ninety degree angles with two long driveways opposite one another. I stare at this cross in the plains and I wonder what will be my sacrifice. Have I already made it, by accepting my own physical barrenness— an extinction of sorts—and moving on? I wonder which animal I am, we are—imperfect and unfinished, or perfect and dangerous—and which, anyway, we should desire to be.

I know how my kame formed, for the back side of the mountain is not like the front. It does not descend, but rather draws into a sinewy, tree-covered twisting mound that turns and snakes off to the west: an esker. Though some sources use the terms kame and esker interchangeably—they are both, after all, depositional post-glacial formations—and they often exist together, they are not the same. In some cases, and I think in this one, an esker creates a kame. The esker, which I have written about before, is what's left of a subglacial stream—all the sediment it carried and deposited over thousands of years—a cast of a stream, if you could make one. And the kame I stand upon is actually the delta of that stream, its triangular deposition, fanning out in all directions. So I'm at the end of the line.

I stand at the top of the kame and look down. It's almost as if I can't see my feet, as if the kame has become me. Its roundness is my belly, hard and unsorted, rootless of trees. I am unhidden without children, like the land below me which has been stripped of its trees and prairie grasses and lies fallow for half of each year. I claim this season as mine, whatever it does or does not bring.

Once, some time ago, I followed the deer path out, stepping over scat, and somewhere at the bottom I was stopped. For a small area of snow had been hooved away, a few inches of soil dug, leaving a small depression. In the center was a whole walnut. Without thinking, I was suddenly on my knees trying to remove it, this buried seed, but my gloved hands and the broken stick I tooled at the dirt could not raise it from the frozen ground. The seed was not mine to take; I had to leave it to be planted or eaten, thinking that for many years to come I would labor over this lesson.

But this spring, on my way to the kame one day, I am stopped by much more than that: I hear machinery that turns both the dog and me around. A week later, when it is finally silent, we hike to the kame to investigate. As predicted, the older pines that had been marked with red blazes have been taken. They lie in a few long piles, next to temporary roads that seem to have changed the forest more—warping the ground, taking out brush, and scraping the bark of numerous standing trees—than the managed cutting. But from the top of the kame, I am surprised to see that at the bottom of the eastern side a large, wide corridor of the mixed deciduous forest has also been taken, much wider than what would be needed just for entering machinery. These trees, too, are being harvested, or perhaps someone is settling on the land that supported them, building their own home at the base of this mountain.

I stand among the downed trees, silent, trying to feel their presence, as I can the live ones. I try to imagine I am at a funeral, but all that I can sense is innately agreeable: the holiday-like aroma of crushed needles, and the scent of fresh-cut wood, with all its potential.

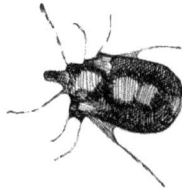

[17] In Praise of Ticks

True to their ability to maintain such a far northern reaching range, wood frogs often hit the water for mating in their vernal pools before the ice has completely melted from the surface, and you can watch them swim underneath as if you are watching something you are about to dream. I have been keeping track of wood frogs, off and on, for many years in many places. On April 2, 2001, in Cornwall-on-Hudson, New York, in my journal, I wrote: Carried a dead otter. No frogs yet. An otter had washed up on the shore of the Hudson River, and I had transported it to the car with the animal curator of the museum at which I worked. But it was really frogs I wanted.

In "Spring," the penultimate chapter of Walden, Thoreau keeps track of the break-up of ice on Walden Pond. He does so not in the descriptive, cerebral, drawn-out sentences that have made his prose so memorable, but in the observational, economical style of the scientist. He writes, "In 1845, Walden was first completely open on the 1st of April; in

'46, the 25th of March; in '47, the 8th of April; in '51, the 28th of March, in '52, the 18th of April, in '53, the 23rd of March, in '54, about the 7th of April." His data spans nine years, and his dates range from March 23, the earliest, to April 18th, nearly a month later. Scientists are now using Thoreau's journals as a starting point in a study that plots changes in the timing of particular spring events, such as the arrival of migrating birds and the flowering of more than 300 plants, in Thoreau's hometown of Concord, Massachusetts. Thoreau's journals, along with a host of other records from nature enthusiasts, as well as the researchers' own five-year study, indicate, they claim, that global warming is occurring.

In 1997, I saw wood frogs on February 19th; in 1998, I saw them around February 11th; in 2001, they had still not appeared by April 2nd, and in 2007, I heard them on March 26th. But my records don't indicate any drastic changes in climate or behavior: global cooling or delayed wood frog mating. Instead, they signify my own movements across the planet, which began in Maryland, where spring happened in February, and have finished here in Wisconsin, where it does not happen until March or April. But wherever I am, and whenever spring is, and whatever it brings, I am always waiting.

There are birds that rear a second brood in mid-July, plants that do not flower until August or September, but spring, with its ever-lengthening light, contains a power that even the original events of other seasons cannot match. Perhaps it is because in spring we feel ourselves inclined toward the source of life: the tilted earth, in orbit, leaning toward the sun. I can predict the date of the first sign of spring for every year to come: December 22nd, for that—depending on the calendar's shift—is when the days begin to get longer again.

My search for wood frogs starts long before it is reasonable to imagine them emerging, when it is, akin to a child's desire to swim in winter, more a memory than anything forthcoming. It is like lost love, in that way, too; even when I begin searching for it again, I feel closer to having experienced it than to ever experiencing it anew. I only know one day I rounded a bend in the trail, and the sound, which I have attempted to record in metaphor many times, came over me: a thousand excited children in rocking chairs on wooden porches, men rising swiftly from benches, women pausing on warped floorboards, trying to remember for what reason they came into a certain room. It is usually a singular, thoughtful sound, but in such great unsynchronized numbers, schizophrenic. It is the sound of wood frogs in a vernal pool, come down from the forest to spawn.

On these early days, when I am searching, although it does not release wood frogs, the oncoming season still flirts, first with flowers that smell like garbage and then a plague of insects, two improbably delightful harbingers of spring. I have seen skunk cabbage, unarguably the first flower—and the first sign altogether, barring day-length—of the season, melting, by its own respiration, the snow which surrounds it as early as December or January. Spathe and spadix push through wetland soil: a tough purple and green streaked hood encloses a pale thumb crowded with petal-less flowers, whose carrion smell attracts pollinators—flies, bees, and stoneflies—which are possibly also enticed to land inside by the warm interior of the entire structure. And then, in

January or February, comes a second nod. On warm, sunny days, especially around the bases of trees, the snow-cover reveals what the soil does not during the rest of the year. Billions of its tiniest inhabitants, called snow fleas or springtails, migrate up to the surface, presumably to feed on decaying leaf litter and sap oozing from trees. Their dark bodies, jumping when frightened, pepper the snow, and it is as if, by their motion, the whole blanket of snow could soon be consumed, ringing in the season.

On March 11th, 2007, I searched for wood frogs too early, and instead found snow fleas by poking a twig at the specks of black in a sunlit patch of old snow until some of them began to move. I finished my hike in mid-afternoon, and the second I stepped onto the road, the second in which my boot arced from the mound of plowed snow onto the wet, clear gravel, a barred owl called from the light behind me. Aware, of course, of the date, I remembered a fitting line from Shakespeare: The bird of night did sit, / even at noonday, upon the market place / hooting and shrieking. Later, I will look up and find that it is not uncommon to hear the barred owl's call, especially the last two notes of the series of eight hoots they normally give, in spring, in daylight hours. Without this information, though, perhaps because of the mindset I am put in during this record-keeping season, perhaps because of the ghost of Julius Caesar, I took it as more than a sign. I took it as a warning.

I marvel at the ease with which I can make this untenable transition, slip into the skin of someone chosen, someone who might hear the bird of night at noon, someone who carried a dead otter, someone who, once, before leaving Maryland, found in the woods in late winter a single deer antler, a gift shed for her there in exactly the center of the trail. That night, my love interest at the time came and spread out on the table in my parents' kitchen the plans to his new house. I remember the special paper and ink, the unrolling as of a scroll, having to weight down the corners, his excitement. And I remember how I hurried him through it, and then produced in my hands my find of the day: the antler, one-half of a pair. He and I wouldn't depart each other for two more years, but could have as easily done it then, so different were the two sets of plans we held in our hands that night.

On the road, after the barred owl warning, I looked down, and sure enough, I had been chosen: I was being parasitized. Treading on my jeans was one other herald of spring: a pair of ticks, looking for their own dark place, for their next blood meal.

I do not have a deep fear of ticks like some of the school children whom I used to teach when I worked at an environmental center. They would get off the bus smelling of Deet already, in hats and long sleeves and pants in even the hottest weather, all the grade-school codes of stylish dress collectively and understandably broken, looking very matter of fact and prepared, as if this was what one did when one visited the forest in the new millennium. Ticks found on children, even just crawling, were supposed to be collected with tweezers and put into plastic bags and kept for parents who could send them, if desired, out to labs for testing.

Ticks have always been parasites, have always been carriers of disease. When I was a child, the worry was over Rocky Mountain spotted fever, a disease about which we knew nothing, but which seemed like it could transport one, polka-dotted and crazy, to distant environs. But it was a vague worry, and we put up only a defensive front, wearing shorts and tee-shirts into the forests and fields, flip-flops or bare feet in the yard. It was only when one of my sisters found a tick on the back of a thigh of another that we were all lined up to have our scalps checked for marauders.

This happened so frequently that finding a tick on my scalp, even now, is a familiar feeling that does not evoke fear or aversion, but something else, like satisfaction, or, at least, confirmed suspicions. It is the feeling of having your fingers stopped by something protruding from your skin that is more foreign than a scab or a mole or a wart, a surface where suddenly your own body stops feeling your fingers on it, an edge you can raise with no sensation except for at one end. I believe I have found ticks in my hair while seated in a high school classroom, discreetly pulled them out, pinched them between thumb and forefinger, and asked to use the bathroom so I could dispose of them. I may even have had a tick discovered during a haircut. It was never an indication of hygiene, simply a measure of time spent in the woods.

Ticks can certainly be dangerous. My husband contracted Lyme disease in the summer of 2006. He spent a week in fever, sweating on the couch, asking me, oddly enough, to take him for walks at ten or eleven at night because he felt he was "not all there" and was afraid to go to sleep. It was as if the disease—a bacteria some ticks pick up from mice and then spread to humans—wanted him to bring another potential host outside where other ticks, and thus other bacteria, might be waiting for them.

I like a slow spring, one that doesn't flood the yard,

but allows each thing to make its singular appearance. Sometimes there is late, accumulating snow and then three or so days of sixty-degree weather that send a deluge of water down-slope, creating temporary shallow lakes out of many acres of soon-to-be-plowed fields on nearby farms, out in the middle of which you may see, surreally, a single white swan, spotless against the mud. These years, the wood frogs, who normally complete their noisy, collective mating within a week and then disappear, silent and separate for the rest of the year, back into the forest, seem to be overtaken by the spring peepers. The spring peepers will mate for over a month, surely until people are sleeping with their windows open, and can hear their ear-splitting call, chirps that sound nearly young enough to be coming from the mouths of the larva themselves, who really can do nothing but hang like quickly waxing crescent moons in their singly laid eggs. There is occasion enough to hear them. I prefer my frogs one at a time.

Perhaps that is why I search for them so early, and find skunk cabbage, and then snow fleas, and then the mourning cloak, spring's second insect, which happens to be, almost unbelievably, a butterfly, one with a purple-brown upper wing lined with blue, irredescent dots and a bright yellow stripe. Mourning cloaks survive winter in an even more remarkable way than in a cocoon, which has always seemed to me a very tenuous room, as it hangs from a leaf-shorn branch by a tiny thread through winter storms. At least the life in the cocoon is nebulous; mourning cloaks overwinter as adults, having to protect the thousands of overlapping scales already on their fully developed wings. They do this by hibernating in tree cavities or rock crevices, then emerge with wings intact when the days first begin to warm.

And then comes the arrival of the birds—the killdeer, phoebe, red-winged blackbird, but first the sandhill crane, with its cavernous wail and throttle, exotic like elephants and artificial as car horns, large and loud as both, which set up shop next to the vernal pool where I await the wood frogs. The cranes stand and stare at the water. Do they know why they are here? Do they remember last year's meal? Are the frogs in the woods—one under every log and root—waiting as well, itching to do something, fully aware of what is next, of where they are going? Or is it just stimulus, response, stimulus, response, all the way down the line? The sun this high in the sky: jump to the shoreline and in. The water this warm: begin calling. Leap from eternal winter to eternal spring. I want to say that is what it is like for me. But that would be a lie. I am always waiting.

The bacteria that causes Lyme disease is a spirochete, a spiral-shaped microbe. The tick itself is not the cause of the disease, but merely the vessel through which some other life, or some other type of being altogether, completes its journey. Lyme disease is only one of many diseases for which the tick is a vector. Ticks can also transmit viruses, other bacteria, parasitic worms, anaplasms, piroplasms, rickettsias and paralytic toxins, all of which, with their multiple syllables, sound horrible. Ticks spread more diversity of diseases than any other arthropod vector.

There are two main families among the 850 species of ticks in the world: soft ticks, and the ones I have been finding on my jeans. These are hard ticks, of the family *Ixodes*, so named because of the tough cuticle that covers their bodies, which keeps them from looking like a raisin, as do some of their softer cousins.

A tick is born into its six-legged larval stage from one of a thousand eggs laid in the leaf litter by a soon-to-die adult female. The tick will eat three meals in its life, and change its clothes three times. In dog ticks and deer ticks, two of the most common ticks to parasitize humans, the first meal usually comes from a rodent. The tick attaches with a backwardly-barbed extension of the mouth called the hypostome. A cement-like substance is secreted from the tick's salivary glands while it is feeding, to help it stay put. This feeding can take, depending on the species of tick, from several days to several months. When the tick is satiated, it will molt and emerge as an eight-legged adult. Ticks are not insects, but arachnids, like spiders.

Some species of ticks fall off their host after the first meal and must find a new host for their second one. Other species will stay on the first host for two meals, or until adulthood. For ticks that fall off, as long as environmental conditions aren't too stressful, several months can pass before a second host is necessary. But any tick in need of a host, be it the first, second, or third, is not simply swept off its feet by whatever happens to walk by next. It chooses its host during a complex waiting behavior that scientists call, rather nobly, "questing."

The first time I heard the sound of wood frogs, many years ago back home in Maryland, I had ventured with my sister west on the railroad tracks, not our usual direction. The sound came from swamps on both sides of us, deafening, alien, from the red water under sedge tents. We knew something was occurring and we weren't ready for it yet—we ran through that section of track with our hands over our ears, in both directions. We were like Miss Walls's student in Seamus Heaney's "Death of a Naturalist:" Every year he borrowed frog eggs from the pond to watch them transform into tadpoles, but one day, when he arrived, " . . . gross-bellied frogs were cocked / on sods; their loose necks pulsed like sails. Some hopped; / The slap and plop were obscene threats. Some sat / poised like mud grenades, their blunt heads farting." Afraid the frogs were waiting for revenge and might pull him in, the boy ran away.

Perhaps the frogs signified change, expectation, and at that time, too young for memory to inform desire, we were more like the sandhill cranes, simply arriving outside with the warmer air. I rediscovered the wood frogs many years later, entered their territory, lifted their sluggish bodies from the cold water framed by ragged edges of ice, and I came to depend on them.

March 26th is the day I first heard wood frogs in 2007 in Wisconsin. I also found that day, later, at home, under my jeans, on the back of my thigh, a tick, latched onto my skin just below my panty-line.

Questing is how a tick finds its host, how that tick found me, from whom it began to receive what the literature always calls, somewhat deliciously, a blood meal. The third blood meal a tick receives must be hearty enough to enable the female to produce eggs. Sometimes the male and female mate on the host after their final meal—I think I have found them this way on my dog. Sometimes they mate after dropping off.

To quest, the tick must possess knowledge of many things—the weather, your height, a chemical you may be leaving around you on the trail like a ghost of yourself. A questing tick will climb to the tip of a piece of grass, or to the edge of a leaf, and wait there with the front two legs extended. Ticks do not jump or propel themselves toward you. Once they have climbed to the proper height—and heights vary with temperature, humidity, and, interestingly, the average height of that particular population of the host species—they simply stop and wait. If you brush by, they will let go with six of their legs and grasp with the exposed two. If you do not, they will continue questing until parched, then return to the more humid soil surface to rehydrate.

Like the lengthening days, the skunk cabbage, the snow fleas, the tick, the mourning cloak , the sandhill crane, you are a sign of spring. You may have heard of pheromones, usually described as chemical signals that are released to attract the opposite sex. Put a cage with a female cecropia moth in it outside at night at the right time, and in the morning you will find it curtained with males, who may have caught a whiff of the pheromone from miles away and traveled as far to reach it, unable to resist. But, as you walk this earth, you are also releasing kairomones, defined as pheromones that attract another organism that has a negative effect on you. Positive and negative are relative terms, remember. You are reaching out in all directions, answering the earth in ways you do not intend and cannot have imagined. You, too, like the gurgle of an early wood frog, are beckoning. You presage something.

I walk all year, but it's true, when the signs of spring

begin to parade themselves I go out more often, lining and relining the air above the trail with my own scent, which will satisfy and confirm a questing tick's suspicions that I am out and about, ready to provide it with what, in its way, it is expecting. I will go out today, whatever this day is, to the place where I saw the wood frogs a year ago. And if they are there, I will find a mossy log, or two hummocks of grass a shoulder's width apart, and balance there with my arms outstretched over the water where, eventually, a pair of eyes may appear as if they are passing from one dimension to another. I want to hold a frog, just for a minute, and then put it back, traipsing through whatever brush it takes to get to it, and whatever I bring out with me, I will only be glad, for we have all been waiting, and we all portend something: the spirochete in the tick, the tick on the beaten grass, the grass beneath the boot, the boot steadying the body that owns the hand that grabs for its host.

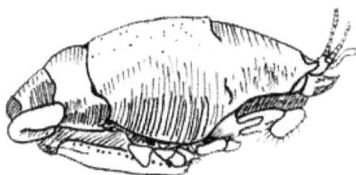

[18] Third Cousins

I sit on the shore between my sister's husband and my own and listen to the place where life began. Here, on the crowded beach, our three blankets nearly touch the blankets of strangers but for the narrow, right-angled avenues of sand we all weave, like settlers, around our parcels of claimed land. I watch children come in from the sea. They search for the patterns of colors on towels and umbrellas that herald, like coats-of-arms, where they belong—with their nuclear families.

Big waves bang the sand. My mother, father, sisters, nieces and nephew have each gone back to his or her campsite, condo, or hotel. So this is my family in this minute: my husband and my brother-in-law. And I do feel them as kin, in spite of what I know about our relatedness—the low percentage of genes we likely share. I feel, finally, with these two men, neither of whom I knew for the first half of my life, a low ripple that connects us, oscillating between blood-relative and stranger. It swells but does not break; with the rest of the family gone, and my husband and I far beyond the medical definition of infertile after four years of trying, no progeny emerge from the surf to join us. Still, the water comes. Love and law are simply the means by which our relationships have been established, but they are not enough to name them. Here, by the sea, I feel something more. I feel myself wavering, however briefly, toward the positive side of a question my husband and I have been considering, mostly individually and mostly subconsciously: adoption.

Soup seems to be the common metaphor in origin of life theories. Often it is preceded by the word "primeval," or the slightly more sinister "primordial," and likely describes an ancient, scummy tide pool where molecules of methane, ammonia, hydrogen sulfide, carbon dioxide or monoxide, and phosphate bobbed around like water-logged saltines. The first to simulate the possible origins of life were a graduate student named Stanley Miller and his professor, Harold Urey. In 1953, the two cooked up their idea of the primordial soup by mixing water, methane, ammonia, and hydrogen in a closed system of glass tubes and flasks into which they fired sparks to simulate lightning. After seven days they found within the flask a "weak, brown soup" containing a few of the twenty-two amino acids that make up the proteins of living cells. Later, similar laboratory experiments by others resulted in the creation of sugars, lipids, and nucleic acids, so that all four classes of biological molecules have been successfully brought forth from various reconstructed primordial soups.

I have never been much a fan of soup, at least not like an earlier love of mine, a man much older than I who could think to save the stock after boiling a chicken, not forget he had put the stock in the freezer, choose and anticipate the day he would thaw it, add carrots, celery, potatoes and noodles, smell it and stir it and simmer it for hours, and then, while eating, emit a very low, infantile purr each time the tilted spoon emptied through his beard-hidden lips. I prefer to chew my food. He dumped me after seven years, and though I was heartbroken, I accepted our split because it made sense; he'd done something that life, when it originated, never could have imagined: he'd had a vasectomy, and even at twenty-two, I knew I wanted children. For me, soup was not enough. Replication was the key to life.

According to the 1995 National Survey of Family Growth, 26% of ever-married women ages 18-44 have considered adoption. Of those 26% who considered it, 16%, or 4% of the total surveyed, actually took steps toward adoption. And of those 16%, 31% completed an adoption. That means that in the United States, in 1995, 1.3% of women ages 18-44 adopted a child.

This statistic seems counter to the subtitle of an article by Evan Eisenberg, writer on nature, culture and technology, published in the online version of Discover Magazine in January of 2001. Eisenberg and his wife, infertile after his wife's cancer, had just adopted a child from China. "Raising someone else's child seems to make no sense from an evolutionary standpoint," Eisenberg's subtitle begins sensibly enough, but then continues glibly, "So why is everyone doing it?" In the article, Eisenberg writes that although official figures do not exist and his figure is only an estimate, 4% of Americans are adopted. He also claims that adoptions have been on the rise since 1950.

But Ellen Herman, faculty member in the department of history at the University of Oregon, founder of the Adoption History Project, and author of Kinship by Design: A History of Adoption in the Modern United States, gives a slightly more conservative estimate. She reports that 5 million Americans alive today are adoptees, which would translate, with the current U.S. population, to just 1.25%, slightly less than a third of Eisenberg's figure. Herman writes that 2-4% of all American families have adopted, and that 2.5% of all children under the age of 18 are adopted. She concurs with Eisenberg that official figures are impossible to find because the national reporting system for adoption, which was wholly voluntary, was in existence for only 30 years—from 1945-1975.

However, contrary to Eisenberg's belief that "everyone is doing it," Herman writes, "Because growing numbers of adoptions are transracial and/or international, many of today's adoptive families have literally made adoption more visible than it was in the past. But total numbers of adoptions have actually declined since 1970." For this assertion she does provide official figures: adoptions have decreased from a peak of 175,000 in 1970, to just 125,000 in recent years. Furthermore, Herman maintains, while adoptions in the past were predominately "stranger" or "non-relative" adoptions, current adoptions—regardless of what appears to be happening—are primarily children adopted by step-parents or biological relatives.

Just how and where that primordial soup capable of

producing all four classes of organic molecules operated is not totally understood or agreed upon—many theories exist, each with its own determinate name: the deep sea vent theory, the iron-sulfur world theory, the radioactive beach hypothesis. But at some point, over hundreds of millions of years, one particular type of molecule gained greater representation in the soup, without will or desire, because of a simple, accidental fact: it could make copies of itself.

Scientists can't be sure exactly how it happened. Richard Dawkins, author of The Selfish Gene, describes it in this way: perhaps each building block in this accidental molecule had an "affinity" for lone pieces of itself that it encountered in the soup, and would stick to them, until it had rebuilt an exact replica. If the replicas were separated, they could then make copies of themselves again. Dawkins calls this special molecule a replicator, titles the book's chapter that chronicles the origins of life "The Replicators," and goes on to stress the importance of the replicator in the thesis of his book: "The replicators that survived were the ones that built survival machines for themselves to live in…they have come a long way, these replicators. Now they go by the name of genes, and we are their survival machines."

My husband and I have tried to replicate our genes through sexual reproduction for what seems a very long time. We have met night after night, through a season of corn, then soy, then corn and soy again, for this thing four years in the making. I have watched the neighbor's tractor's light move steadily toward us and worried that the driver might see. But when the rows end he turns his machine, before the light reaches into our bedroom. We move to the unnatural music of the irrigators on their hinged orbits, which arc, spread-eagle, over what grows where the farmer has brought the deep to the surface. And always, before it is over, comes the stench—not the wild spoil of a single skunk, or the musk of one garter snake—but the crowded stench of Holsteins, hooves in their own excrement, udders mottled with over-rich soil.

Sex has failed me. But it has been useful in the evolution of life on earth.

The first survival machines were likely Dawkin's replicator surrounded by some sort of membrane. This, the prokaryotic cell, did not reproduce by having sex. Instead, its replicator, which in present life we know as DNA—a long strand of genes—made copies of itself through either binary fission or budding. Both of these replicating methods still occur today in organisms such as archaea, bacteria, and protists, and even in some plants and animals. In both binary fission and budding, the first step is for the DNA inside the cell to duplicate. In binary fission, the cell splits into two small copies of itself; in budding, a new cell grows outs of the original cell and then gets larger. With the exception of the occasional copying errors that drive evolution, in both binary fission and budding the newly created cells are 100% identical to each other, hardly daughters, although that is what they are often called.

True daughters, as well as sons, parents, grandparents, siblings and aunts and uncles, did not come along until after the appearance of eukaryotic cells—cells with a neatly bound nucleus. It was the eukaryotes that evolved sexual reproduction. This was about 1.2 billion years ago, 2.8 billion years after the first prokaryote appeared. Genes want to replicate themselves, but sometimes, especially in times of uncertain conditions, it is better for a parent to have children who are slightly variable, rather than all clones of each other and their creator. Then, a single disease won't necessarily kill all of them.

Sexual reproduction allows for this variability in two ways: first during meiosis, and then during fertilization. Meiosis is the creation of sperm and egg cells in the male and female, each of which contains half of the genes of a viable offspring. During meiosis, something called "crossover" occurs, when genes swap positions on their corresponding chromosomes, so that no offspring inherits a chromosome that is completely identical to the chromosomes in either of its parents or any of its siblings, past, present, or future. Then, during fertilization, sperm and egg combine the genetic information from two members of the species. The result is a unique individual who shares exactly 50% of his genes with his mother, and 50% with his father, but has them arranged uniquely on his or her chromosomes.

At the beach, my mother and my oldest sister refuse to swim. My mother doesn't even wear a bathing suit. They are done with the ocean, its stew of exposed bodies and broken shells and jelly fish. But the rest of us are all in it: my oldest sister's eleven-year-old son and two teenaged daughters, my husband, me, my other sister, her husband and their two little girls, even my father. My youngest niece is three; she bobs around in her life jacket, only her head above water, swimming between swells from adult to adult. But her sister, the six-year-old, I am impressed to find, like her older cousins, has abandoned all flotation devices in favor of the natural buoyancy of her own body. I crouch next to her so that we are the same height, and in water up to our necks, we doggy-paddle through the swells together. She laughs as the water pushes and pulls; I worry that it might suck her under. When a big wave crests right on top of us, she reaches for me and I lift her up. When it passes, we separate. The adults offer her advice. Keep your mouth closed. Keep your eye on the waves. Don't turn your back on the ocean.

My sister exits the water, arms at her sides, no longer holding her younger daughter. My niece hangs down the front of her mother's body, dangling like a pendant, her hands clasped tightly behind her mother's neck. My sister turns to me from the beach and says, "Look at this necklace. I thought I liked it when I bought it at the store, but now I'm not so sure; I can't get it off." They are both smiling.

Except for my eleven-year-old nephew, who can stay in the ocean for hours, we gradually make it back to the towels. We look changed; our wet hair coils around the salt and sand it carries. We lie on backs, bellies, and sides around my mother and oldest sister, who sit under two umbrellas. They inform us they have dubbed this vacation our twenty-year reunion, for the year is 2008, and the last time my mother, father, and my two sisters and I made the three-and-a-half hour journey together from our home in central Maryland to the ocean was in 1988. But the family my parents created has expanded. They now have three sons-in-law and five grandchildren. My sisters and I are aunts, in addition to daughters. My sisters are mothers.

When we were here before, just the five of us, we were a tight-knit group with each member sharing 50% of his genes with at least three others—my sisters and I were 50% related to everyone. Only my mother and father, to each other, were genetically strangers. A nuclear family—two parents and their offspring—are a snug bunch, bound by shared experiences on the outside, yes, but also by their first shared experience—that of developing from the same genes. But now we are a mix of all kinds of degrees of relatedness.

Determining your relatedness to family members is easy. "It could be useful," Richard Dawkins writes in a moment of wit during The Selfish Gene, "in writing your will." Let's say you want to determine your relatedness to your sister's child, your niece. First, trace your family tree back to the most recently born common ancestor you both share. In this case it would be your mother (your niece's grandmother) and your father (your niece's grandfather.) Select one of those common ancestors, and count the steps on the family tree it takes to get from you, through that ancestor, to your niece. In this case, it would be three: up to your mother, down to your sister, then down to your niece. Each step on the family tree is equal to ½. Now, take ½ to the power of the number of steps you counted. In this case, ½ (3) or ½ x ½ x ½ = 1/8. But since you share two common ancestors with your niece, you must multiply your result, 1/8, by two, giving you ¼. You share ¼ of your genes (beyond the baseline of the 90 or so percent of genes that you share with all other members of your species) with your niece.

So, you share ½ of your genes with your mother, father, daughter, son, sisters, and brothers (the number for siblings is an average; in actuality it can be slightly more or slightly less than one half, or in the case of identical twins, 100%). You share ¼ of your genes with your aunts, uncles, nieces, nephews, grandchildren, and grandparents, and 1/8 with your first cousins, great-grandparents and grand-nieces and nephews. Interestingly, a third cousin, Dawkins writes, shares about 1/128 of your own genes, which is about as related to you as anyone in the general population.

There are ways to replicate your genes other than sexual reproduction. Scientists discovered this while trying to explain altruism—when an animal acts in such a way as to decrease its own fitness while increasing the fitness of others. There are many examples of apparent altruism in the animal kingdom: warning behaviors, food-sharing, even, occasionally, adoption. But if animals are survival machines created for the replication of their own genes, why would they ever risk their own lives in order to help another organism?

In groups of Belding's ground squirrels, which are native to the mountains of the Western United States, squirrels can often be seen standing near their burrows, alertly watching for predators both in the sky and on the ground, while other nearby squirrels forage in the grass. When a predator is seen, the watchers emit a loud alarm call, which has been observed to draw the predator's attention to the calling squirrel, even sometimes leading to an attack. On the surface, this seems very altruistic: the foraging squirrels can run for cover while the sentinel squirrel takes the heat.

But researchers found that alarm calls were not consistent among all Belding's ground squirrels. Females were more likely to emit alarm calls than males. This makes sense, considering the fact that females live among relatives while males leave their natal territories and do not live near their kin. When they give predator-warnings, female Belding's ground squirrels are, in effect, ensuring the survival of multiple relatives who will produce offspring that share a percentage of their genes. Further supporting this, reproductive females whose living sisters, daughters, or granddaughters were nearby were more likely to call than reproductive females who had no such living relatives. In addition, reproductive females defended their territory less aggressively against relatives than against unrelated females, cooperatively defended adjacent territories when they belonged to related females, but did not defend the territories of neighbors who were not related, even when they had lived next to one another for two years or more.

The conclusion is that most animals exhibit altruism only in the presence of kin, and that although an animal may appear to risk its own life in the short-term, by increasing the likelihood of the survival of its closely related kin, it is really, as a survival machine, ensuring that its genes will be passed on (through its kin) into the next generation. Martin Daly and Margo Wilson, in Sex, Evolution, and Behavior, call organisms "evolved nepotists with benign inclinations toward their relatives." The only catch is that the cost to the actor needs to be less than the degree of relatedness of the beneficiary multiplied by the relative's benefit. This is known as Hamilton's rule, named after the man who proposed it, and is often expressed as the equation $c < rb$. In other words, organisms should be willing to die only for more than two of their brothers, and no less than nine of their cousins.

So, that day at the beach, lifting my niece above the breaking waves, worrying that she might get water in her nose were, in one sort of way, the 25% of our genes that we share calling out to one another.

Current statistics show, as stated earlier, that somewhere between 2 and 4% of Americans are adopted. But in some cultures of Oceania—a region in the Pacific Ocean that includes Australia, New Zealand, Papua New Guinea, and the islands of Polynesia, Melanesia, and Micronesia— the percentages are much higher. Among the Manini of Tuamotu Arch and the Tahiti of Society Island, 25% of the population has been adopted. Among the Maat of New Hebrides, the percentage of adopted children jumps to 31%. And among the Kapingamarangi of the Carolina Islands, the percentage of adopted children is an astonishing 54% of the total population. What would drive a human population to this ultimate act of altruism—providing food, shelter, care and love to a strange child, forcing your own progeny to share the resources you could afford them with siblings who did not share 50% of their genes, and perhaps increasing the number of children the strange child's parents could have and decreasing the number you could have because you were busy raising their child?

In 1977, Joan B. Silk, in "Adoption and Kinship in Oceania," gathered the data which showed that the high majority of these adoptions, as you may have guessed, like the adoptions in America, are adoptions of kin. In the Manini, 84% of the adoptions were of kin; in the Tahiti and the Maat 93% were, and among the Kapingamarangi, 97% of the adoptions were of biological relatives. Furthermore, most adoptions were of closely related relatives; in all eleven societies that Silk studied, over half of the adoptions were of kin related by ¼ to their adopters. Most of these adoptions, in other words, were simply aunts and uncles taking in their nieces and nephews. Silk also found that, in two-thirds of the societies, biological children were allocated larger shares of their parents' estates than their adopted siblings.

If the altruistic acts of humans can be reduced to such selfish terms, so, certainly, can the seemingly altruistic acts of our animal-brothers. When a lactating elephant seal's pups are killed, she will often adopt a pup who is not related to her. As it turns out, the mother must complete her lactation cycle in order to become pregnant again the following year. Her nourishment of the alien pup is less an example of altruism than a clear course toward ensuring that she will again produce her own offspring.

Still, as Dawkins points out, sometimes monkey mothers who have lost a child will steal a baby from another mother and raise it. Because this frees that mother up to produce another child, and delays the originally bereaved mother from producing her own offspring, such an act is doubly unproductive for the bereaved mother's genes. This has lead Dawkins to call adoption a "misfiring of a built-in rule... a mistake that happens too seldom for natural selection to have 'bothered' to change the rule by making the maternal instinct more selective." Wilson and Daly's statement on adoption in the animal world is just slightly less dismal. They write that successful adoption can occur, but only by "'tricking' psychological mechanisms whose evolved function is to direct parental feeling discriminatively to own offspring."

At the beach, my niece and her father began digging for Atlantic mole crabs—sand fleas, they called them—small, convex, fast-moving crabs with no pincers that come in with high tide, then burrow into the sand backwards until the next high tide takes them out again. I had never seen them before. My brother-in-law, always a trickster, threw a few of the egg-shaped crabs at me, aiming for the scooped neck of my suit. His daughter filled a bucket with sand and water and handfuls of them. The bucket sat on the beach by our towels, but a few hours later, the water warmed and the crabs began to float to the surface. My sister, worried they might be dying, carried her daughter's bucket to the shore and released the crabs back into the ocean.

What is it like to be a parent? I, only a daughter, wife, and aunt, cannot tell you. I can observe my sisters with their children. I can try to multiply the love I feel for my nieces and nephew by two. But to convey this feeling, I must use the words of other writers who happen also to be mothers. In Annie Dillard's recent novel The Maytrees, Lou Bigelow recalls, after the birth of her only child, how her mother had quipped, on the day of Lou's wedding to Toby Maytree, that Lou would never know true love until she had a baby. Her mother, it turns out, was right. The immensity of Lou's feelings toward her son Petie is unpredicted and unparalleled: "She never put him down. She must feel his skin on her, feel his cranium in her arm's crook, his belly on her belly, and smell his breath, his scalp, . . . They were pieces of each other foully parted. When they had to separate, she took ever-deeper breaths as if air had no use. Her sternum and her ventral torso and arms ached. Maytree had some horseshoe magnets in the kitchen. She gave each a wrench to hold."

Lou's body almost cannot function properly without her son near. The love she feels for him, as a new mother, is jarring, but it is also innate, so rudimentary it is compared even to magnetism, one of the four fundamental forces of the universe. Sometimes I think I should be able to relate. After all, I am a daughter. I share 50% of my genes with each of my parents. But it is they, my mother and father, who are the magnets, the ones who ache. I am just a solitary piece of metal, as unable as a wrench to conjure up the kind of love a parent must feel for his or her offspring.

When I held my niece above the waves, what were our 25% of shared genes saying to one another? Just how does that affinity that Dawkins' original replicator felt for its own building blocks translate to the relationship between my niece and me? How do we recognize our own kin? And conversely, what might be lacking in the relationship I might have with an adopted child?

In Lasioglossum zephyrum, a type of sweat bee native to North America, each spring, a single pregnant queen founds a nest in a burrow in the ground. Several of her daughters leave the nest, mate, and return. Sometimes, unrelated pregnant queens will try to gain access to the nest, but they are stopped by worker bees which guard the entrance to the burrow with their bodies and frisk the bees who try to enter with chemically sensitive antennae. When researchers bred bees in the lab with varying degrees of relatedness, they found that the more closely related a guard bee was to a would-be entrant, the more likely he was to let that bee into the burrow.

In A Natural History of Parenting, Susan Allport writes that in addition to all the gazing that occurs between newborn and mother, just one day after giving birth, mothers are able to identify a hungry, crying infant as their own. Just six hours after birth, sixty-one percent of mothers can distinguish their infant solely by smell. Does love begin simply as a sound wave, a scent on a molecule that passes between two people?

My sisters and I used to play a game in the ocean. We called it "egg." One of them—they usually played this role because I was always a little afraid—would curl into a ball, hold her knees to her chest and tuck her head under. The other person, standing in waist-deep water, would roll the egg sideways, push it to the bottom, and turn it end-over-end, until the egg had to come up for breath. The ocean was a third player; the ebb and flow of the waves and the fluctuating depth caused the egg to lose all sense of direction, become part of the sea again. I play egg with my husband now, but I push too hard in water that is too shallow, and he comes up bleeding. His shoulder has scraped the sand.

If my husband and I bring our ambivalence over adoption to the surface, if we decide to adopt a child, to trick ourselves into being parents, the child will share 1/128 of my genes. It will be as related to me as my great-great grandmother's great-great grandchild. At first, this seems like a comfort. But when I ask my parents for a name, if they can identify a third cousin of mine on our family tree, I get no response. I realize that an adopted child will also be as related to me as my brother-in-law, or my husband, or, for that matter, anyone who surrounded us on the crowded shore that day those great incubating ocean waves sent a feeling of kinship through the air. Will I see the child as a stranger or recognize it as my third cousin? And what is the difference? Just words.

So I leave it at that. Perhaps we will find each other, my

little third cousin, and perhaps we will not. Whichever way it happens I will be fine. This, you see, is the grace in my situation: I cannot possibly know what I am missing. And, I am sure you are thinking, if you are already a biological mother or father, this is the pitiable sadness of it also.

[19] *Limnology*

I release the weight of my head, an other-worldly, inhuman feeling, leaning back until my hairline is completely submerged. I must move my eyes to the top of their sockets in order to see the earth. Floating here, I barely rise above the surface. I am not an island; instead, my outline pushes at the water as if it were land, my breath and occasional tread producing tiny waves that seem to etch my own container. The water rims my face and body in such a way that the lake which surrounds me becomes the shore. And I become myself again, what I mostly am: a body of water.

I first performed this ritual—this barely moving backfloat—many years ago in a Green Mountain pond while on vacation in Vermont. After only two weeks, the tannin in that pond would split the ends of my hair and stain it for the rest of the summer. My hair would soften, too; even after returning to my home in Maryland I would run my hands down the back of my head, and it was like touching the lightly jelled roots of pond lilies beneath the surface; I felt like I couldn't shed that pond's water.

This new thing—pond-swimming—was not like the quick, cleansing dips I had taken in the water of streams all my life, water that seemed to scrub as it washed over me. In that cold, spring-fed knot, that red mountain cyst, I first learned about still water, about how it stays with you, instead of going forward. Later, when I moved to lake country, leaving streams behind indefinitely, I would slowly come to realize that as inconceivable as the loss of one thing can be, just as unthinkable may be the survival of another.

When I moved to Wisconsin from Maryland, the following became one of my mantras: Maryland has no natural lakes. I said it because it made me sound happy to be around them, these results of glaciation or other geologic or geomorphic processes; acknowledging lakes, proclaiming them special from a foreigner's perspective, I quickly found, was a way to make friends instead of enemies. But what I was really saying when I admitted this, when I stood next to these cavities in the earth that opened up acres or more of forest, which were impossible to overlook when one came upon them while hiking, was that I missed the small, veiled, but certain presence of moving water.

Four of the arteries streaming blood toward my Great-Aunt Edna's 86-year-old heart have become clogged, despite the fact that she has been on a low-cholesterol diet for thirty years, subsisting mainly on the fruits and vegetables of her own garden: cherries and strawberries, cucumbers and peppers. Her doctor told her, as we so often hear in heart disease cases, that she was a walking time bomb. He told her this after she had spent the morning canning a tomato harvest. A week later, she went in for a quadruple-bypass. Most doctors won't operate on a woman this old but Aunt Edna's daughter found one who would, because Aunt Edna wanted the surgery.

In bypass surgery, the doctor breaks the breastbone and stops the patient's heart. While a machine keeps the patient's blood circulating, the doctor takes a blood vessel from elsewhere in the body—usually a leg—and uses it to create a bypass around the blocked portion of the artery. One end is attached to the aorta—the heart's main artery— and the other end is attached to the clogged artery below the point of blockage, creating a new pathway for the blood to flow through on its way to the heart. I imagine the blockages in Aunt Edna's chest before the operation as natural dams, impoundments with the potential to end her life. Then, after the doctor has stapled her together again, I see them as four stagnant oxbow lakes left by mature streams as they maneuvered new channels.

The weekend Aunt Edna went in for surgery, her daughter gave my parents the last of the sweet corn from her garden. But it was too tough, and neither of them could eat it. Perhaps she'd planted early corn, my mother told me over the phone, and now, now, it was very late in the season.

I have become a limnologist, one who studies fresh water. This study comes not as a profession, and not from a love of the easy, alveolar glides I must perform with my tongue to produce the words that limnology involves: lotic and lentic. I study lakes now out of necessity. I grew up near lotic, or flowing, waters. The Maryland Department of Natural Resources' website on bays and streams asks: "Did you know that everyone in Maryland lives within minutes of a stream?" It's true—out our back door was the East Branch of the Patapsco River, and out our front door was the West. But presently I live in a lentic, or still-water, environment. To Maryland's zero natural lakes, Wisconsin has 13,120.

It seems easy to know all there is about lakes. My physical geography book gives lakes two pages; rivers and streams get an entire chapter. Lakes occur at low points. Their distinguishing characteristic is that their input—be it from spring-water or groundwater seepage—is greater than their output. Lakes fill in. They entrap. Inflow brings sediment, and outflowing streams—if they exist—cut deeper and deeper channels, draining water. Both of these processes gradually make the lake shallower. The development of soil allows for an increase in plant growth and animal life. Then, there are more things dying: scales and chitin, grass and bone settle on the lakebed. And death, too, raises the bottom.

Although I am a lover of streams, of channels, of banks, of the coursing of water, it is the opposite of this—the blockage of flow—as evidenced by Aunt Edna, which runs in my family. Heart trouble is common on my mother's mother's side. My relatives' blood, for whatever reason, carries too much cholesterol—like the blood of millions of Americans—which builds up in their arteries, causing the arteries to narrow and harden, and eventually to slow down or block off blood flow to the heart.

My great grandmother had several heart attacks before she died. My mother's Aunt Helen and Aunt Pearl both died

of heart trouble; Aunt Pearl had a bypass at age 68. Mother's
Uncle Bud, who knew he had heart problems but never had
health insurance, also died of a heart attack. And mother's
Uncle Dave, an avid hunter who eventually could not walk
around in the woods because it made him so out of breath,
has had two bypasses—his first was at age 40. This seems like
a lot, my mother says, but there were thirteen siblings, and
although all of them have high cholesterol, the rest are all
now in their 80's and 70's. She says it like that, in that order,
80's and then 70's, as if these aunts and uncles are actually
getting younger, as if, because of the continued passing of
blood through their veins, they are somehow becoming more
alive.

As a limnologist, I compare and contrast my stream and
lake knowledge.

A stream goes by you. You happen upon it, a trickle
at the bottom of a hill. You cross it, then cross back, then
cross again, stitching yourself to its progress. You build
dams, place stepping stones; it builds dams, fells logs that
you cross on. You watch it muddy and clear as you rearrange
its channel, sometimes on purpose, sometimes by accident.
A stream is a path.

But a lake, a lake sits with you. Following its edge will
only bring you back to your beginning. It takes you to itself.
It reveals a moose.

You squat in a stream. You do not swim. Where it is
deep enough, you raft, watching the occasional head of a
water snake, like the curved, black end of the staff of some
underwater chief, angle away from you. You wade, shoeless,
the arches of your bare feet aching from the occasional

oblong stone, or with the tongues of your battered sneakers lapping up the river's suspended load to rub against your midfoot. You duck under barbed wire or electric fence that whaps the small of your back so that you make an animal sound which, once you've cleared the wire and realize you've only been shocked and not killed, loudens into a laugh.

A lake, though, a lake holds you up. It is sometimes inaccessible, surrounded by marsh or swamp. Often, it will let you enter from only one point, which you have the challenge of finding. And sometimes, you abhor its bottom. Not always, but sometimes you would not put your foot down in a lake for fear of disappearing. On the other hand, in response to even the smallest underwater movements of your arms and legs, a lake will support you; it will hold you up.

A stream orients. I have stood at the 45th parallel on the Eau Claire River in Wisconsin, looked north exactly 45 degrees to the pole and south exactly 45 degrees to the equator. I felt equal, halved. I knew where I was on the planet. I have stood along the Mississippi in Hannibal, Missouri and looked upstream to Minnesota, and downstream to the Gulf of Mexico. I could feel the Appalachians to the east and the plains to the west, the roundness of the earth, how a stream both divides and connects.

But a lake, its water often seeping up, links you only to the underworld. In the winter, a lake can bury you. Or, you can glide, ghost-like, above it.

A stream brings you closer to something or away. It cuts the earth and the ball of your foot with a piece of what will soon be sea glass. It trickles, babbles, riffles, rushes, roars, froths, riffles, falls, and then meanders. A stream can surprise you by sight, but if you listen, it calls you from a distance. If you follow it, a stream will give you answers.

A lake is silent, but its silence is undermined by its size. Once it's spotted you can't imagine having missed it. And a lake, a lake breeds questions. Who knows if you could swim across, how deep it is, or what lurks beneath its surface.

In Greek mythology, the world of the living was separated from the world of the dead by five rivers. Styx, the river of hate, is often thought to be the one which Charon ferried souls across on their way to the underworld. But it was actually across the river Acheron, the river of woe, where Charon docked his boat. There, Cerberus, the dragon-headed dog, guarded the gates of Hades so that no one who entered could leave again. But whether it was Styx or Acheron, I've never quite been able to assimilate this metaphor. I just can't see the river as a one-way border.

The other side of the river in which my sisters and I played in Maryland was steep and rocky. From our perspective, the dark between the rocks on this opposite side always looked like deep caves. We suspected they held what we could not find along our own bank: perfectly formed quartz crystals, midden piles from early humans, wall etchings of animals long extinct. But when we waded across, or crossed on a fallen log, and climbed the rocks, their cracks became barely large enough for a fox den, similar in size to the cracks in the very rocks we had stumbled down to get to our own side of the river. It was all the same, and getting home was as easy as crossing back over when we thought it was time for dinner.

I have always found as a more rational mode of transport

to the underworld the way that Dionysus took when he went
to rescue his dead mother, Semele. Semele had been im-
pregnated with Dionysus by Zeus, but was filled with doubt
about the true identity of her child's father when jealous
Hera, disguised as an old crone, told her it could not possibly
be Zeus. To end her doubt, Semele asked Zeus to reveal
himself to her in his true godly form. When he did, of
course, she died from a lightning bolt. Zeus saved the child,
still a fetus, by sewing him into his thigh. Later in his life,
Dionysus, known as the "twice-born," retrieved his mother
from Hades, but he did not sneak his way across a simple
river to do it. Instead, Dionysus reached the underworld
in a way that makes perfect sense to me: by diving into a
bottomless lake.

Once, my parents took us to the place where the East
and West Branches of the Patapsco River joined, a place
where they had both swum as children. The East Branch
squeezed under a railroad bridge, bulged for a hundred yards
or so where it joined with the West Branch, and then the
two of them together were pinched beneath a second bridge,
which held Patapsco Road, to form the North Branch. It
was not a lake, this coagulant of rivers between two bridges,
and it was hardly bottomless, but unlike any other place we
knew along these rivers, here, the water was over our heads.
Also, while usually the water ran clear, revealing beds of min-
now-colored skipping stones and the tiny crayfish that lived
under them, at this place you could not see the bottom. My
parents told us that when they were little there had been a
large rock that you could stand on in the middle of the con-
fluence, but I didn't want to find it. This was before I could
swim, and I stayed close to the east bank of the East Branch,

jumping through the water with arms outstretched, afraid that if I went too deep I might, like Dionysus, enter a world far different than the one I was in, or the one I could see on the other side of the river, a world I might not be able to rise from again.

Waiting for death should be like the anticipation of snow: the initial forecast a prognosis, something exciting and not unexpected but that nonetheless doesn't happen very often, something to be talked about with friends and even acquaintances, like we shared with shaking heads the doctor's decree that Aunt Edna was a walking time bomb. The scrutiny of reports from multiple meteorologists—one thinks the storm might move a hair north and bury us all—could be like the gathering of second opinions, a way to pass the time before what we know will come, what we hope with our stalwart strength and heroic idealism will be a bigger storm than the storms that have hit us in the past or have hit anyone we know. The repeated checking through blinds and partially opened storm doors for the snow's beginning against the light of a single porch bulb would be like a physician's final examinations. And then would occur the silent and utter solitary commencement of the snow.

We need to turn our fear of death, our notion that death is a departure, a voyage, to another feeling entirely. We need to trust that, like snow which falls all night and all day, and keeps us from school, work, shopping, walking a favorite path, death will, in its own way, keep us here too. Death does not transport. It does not flow. Like a lake, death holds.

Although the land of my youth was canvassed with lotic

waters, I did know some lakes before I moved to Wisconsin. One summer, instead of swimming at the local pool, my family swam at Cascade Lake, a dammed tributary of the East Branch of the Patapsco. But we only swam there one season, unsettled by the feel of our finely silted skin whenever we surfaced, as if we could never fully emerge from the water.

In high school, late one summer night, a friend and I and twin boy classmates went for a swim in Prettyboy Reservoir. We stripped to our underwear and tennis shoes. They jumped in from a rock overhang; more cautious, I slipped in below. We returned to our car to find a parking ticket. The next morning, we were discovered again; I had to confess where I'd been and what I'd been doing when my mother commented on the strong smell of decomposition emanating from my shoes.

Before my husband and I moved to Wisconsin, we lived on a lake in Pennsylvania. There are 2,500 bodies of water in Pennsylvania that are considered lakes; 2,450 of them were man-made. Pennsylvania's 50 natural lakes are all filled kettles, holes made from latent or buried chunks of ice left as the most recent glacier receded. Forty-three of these kettles occur in the Poconos, in the Northeastern corner of the state, precisely where my husband and I lived for a few years after we married. But the lake we lived on—Nyce Lake—like Cascade Lake and Prettyboy Reservoir, was unnatural. It had been made by damming one of the many beautiful creeks that trickle over the red, rocky Pocono plateau.

As a result, this lake was shallow and always tugged at the bottom of my canoe, the stumps of the razed trees refusing to give up their state of being; in their minds, they were solid and tall still, confused at how the air around them had thickened, how things glided past them or clung, instead of perched or excavated within, how wings had devolved back into fins. When we swam in Nyce Lake, as in Cascade Lake, we emerged suited in silt, the ridges in our own skin flooded with what the lake had held.

Two people have died this year. Aunt Edna was not one of them. In fact, she used the least amount of post-op medication, the doctor says, that he has ever witnessed. She is teaching us that we, too, can go through this, my mother says; we learn from our elders.

The two who died were both inconceivably young: the first, seventeen, a former student; the other, thirty-one, a friend from childhood. Both passages were quick and presumably painless, both collapses, one during track practice, the other while sipping a martini with friends on a visit to Chicago. The deaths were described by the obituaries as unexpected, sudden. They were probably unfelt, unrealized by the passers-away. But they were a shock to the rest of us.

Autopsies published in the newspaper and shared on email told us more about them than we know about the living: a weak heart, an enlarged liver, fluid in the lungs. This information, and my desire to know it, reminded me of a picture of my niece before she was born, an ultrasound my family passed around and also watched on video, during which the fetus turned her unclosed head directly toward the camera. My mother, as anxious as anyone to meet this new addition to the family, interpreted the movement for all of us: it's like she knows we shouldn't be doing this. Perhaps we're not meant to see beneath the surface.

For months, after I moved to Wisconsin, no longer minutes from streams, I stared at the map trying to find them, and I discovered a new word: flowage. The word itself is beautiful. By sound alone, it seems to pair with lotic. It implies movement, is defined as the act of flowing or the state of being flooded. There was the Brule River Flowage, the Chippewa River Flowage, the Turtle-Flambeau Flowage. It seemed almost every river had one. I imagined it was a way to emphasize, in this land of 13,120 natural lakes (15,081 lakes total), that these were lotic waters. On the map, the flowages were shaped like splattered paint along bulging sections of river. What would cause river water to spread out this way, I wondered, and then regather itself?

Finally, I recognized these flowages for what they truly were: man-made reservoirs. They were dammed rivers; water that wanted to be on the move held back, currents reduced. They were nothing more than what had made my shoes stink, giving me away after a night of teen-aged freedom in Maryland so long ago. I can't understand why a land with a surplus of lakes would dam all of its rivers, but hardly a river in the country isn't dammed, and each one comes with its own creation story, its own logical reasons: hydroelectric plants, paper mills, flood protection, recreation. One website calls the Turtle-Flambeau Flowage a "wilderness gem." But flowages, which push water back up the main river channel and up the channels of feeder streams, really make these wilderness areas look, from above, like a tree with a diseased branch, fattened with burls.

I visit Maryland and my family plans a trip to Cunningham Falls State Park. We'll hike to the falls and have a picnic.

I'm excited to be in the mountains again, to walk along a stream that rushes and trips out of them. After lunch, we take the kids swimming in Hunting Creek Lake. It's packed. The water is warm, and even fifty yards out, it's barely up to our waists. Where it finally gets deep enough to swim, my feet scrape the bottom. I can feel colder water passing beneath me, and below it, a thick lane of leaf litter, which my father and I decide must be the path of the original stream, the impoundment of which has created this lake. It is hard to come up from beneath the water without bits of black bark on your forehead and arms. I'm disgusted, but no one else seems bothered.

And then a voice comes out of me, so unforeseen I hardly believe it is my own. It tells them, my mother and my father and my sisters, my nieces and nephew, about a lake I have come to know. It is a lake in Wisconsin, I say, a natural lake, with a pebbled bottom as unsoiled as if the ice had just finished its carving and depositing, with water as cold and clear as if you were swimming in glacial melt itself.

I will not lie. When I sit by a lake in Wisconsin, I still want to stretch it into a stream. I want to doctor it, remove some earth, raise one end, and fray that end into tiny feeder creeks. I want to split it like the tannin-filled first natural lake that I swam in split the ends of my hair, and would have split them to the root had I continued to swim there. It's not that I want a river in order to get somewhere, to travel along or even to cross; I just want to sit by it and know where I am.

I imagine I can make streams like we make lakes, unclot this earth, fill its veins, keep it alive. Lakes are for the unborn and the dead. I am neither of these. I am alive, but no matter where I am, no matter what I believe I need to survive, no matter how much it pains me to say it, I have lakes of a sort in my blood. I cannot deny it. I am a lake; I am a body of water surrounded by land.

At Christmas, I say hello to Aunt Edna in church. She's doing well. The nurses are nice; they have to tell her to slow down on the treadmill at therapy. She did trip and fall somewhere, and she's retaining water in her hand from that. She shows it to me, her right hand, fat like a baby's. But six months have passed, and every day, she says, she's feeling better.

Apprentice House is the country's only campus-based, student-staffed book publishing company. Directed by professors and industry professionals, it is a nonprofit activity of the Communication Department at Loyola University Maryland.

Using state-of-the-art technology and an experiential learning model of education, Apprentice House publishes books in untraditional ways. This dual responsibility as publishers and educators creates an unprecedented collaborative environment among faculty and students, while teaching tomorrow's editors, designers, and marketers.

Outside of class, progress on book projects is carried forth by the AH Book Publishing Club, a co-curricular campus organization supported by Loyola University Maryland's Office of Student Activities.

Eclectic and provocative, Apprentice House titles intend to entertain as well as spark dialogue on a variety of topics. Financial contributions to sustain the press's work are welcomed. Contributions are tax deductible to the fullest extent allowed by the IRS.

To learn more about Apprentice House books or to obtain submission guidelines, please visit www.apprenticehouse.com.

Apprentice House
Communication Department
Loyola University Maryland
4501 N. Charles Street
Baltimore, MD 21210
Ph: 410-617-5265 •F ax: 410-617-2198
info@apprenticehouse.com
www.apprenticehouse.com